IN THE SHADE
OF A FLOWER

POEMS

[WITH SELECTED FRENCH VERSIONS]

BY

JEAN-YVES SOLINGA

FIRST EDITION

Little Red Tree Publishing, LLC,
635 Ocean Avenue, New London, CT 06320

Other books by Jean-Yves Solinga

Clair-Obscur of the soul (2008)
Clair-Obscur de l'âme (2009)

DEDICATION

It is with the support of my wife Elaine, my children Robert and Nicole and among friends that I continue to find the meaning of writing. They have helped me live and prosper in two cultures and languages and get inspiration in both.

Copyright © 2009 Jean-Yves Solinga

All photographs used inside this book are by the kind permission of Jean-Yves Solinga and each photograph is attributed accordingly.

Illustrations on pages 18, 76, 106 and 115 are by Katy Norman.

Manufactured in USA
First Edition 2009

Cover and Book Design:
Michael John Linnard, MCSD

The following quotations and passages used in this book are by kind permission:

Page xii: Quotes from Gustave Flaubert
Page 28: Passage from *Le roi se meurt* [*Exit the King*], by Eugène Ionesco.
Pages 31 & 34: Passage from *La nausée,* by Jean-Paul Sartre.
Page 36: Two verses from "Ballade des dames du temps jadis," by François Villon.
Page 55: Two quotes from an article in *The Chronicle Review*, Section B, March 20, 2009 by David P. Barash.
Page 73: Passage from *Ne me quitte pas,* by Jacques Brel
Pages 122 & 124: Three passages from *The Little Prince*, by Antoine de Saint Exupéry
Pages 126 & 127: Passage from *L'invitation au voyage*, by Charles Baudelaire
Pages 126 & 127: Passage from *Chéri*, by Colette

The poem "Réflexions sur l'Olympia de Manet," page 63, was first published by Little Red Tree Publishing, in *Clair-obscur de l'âme* (2009) by Jean-Yves Solinga.

Library of Congress Cataloging-in-Publication Data

Solinga, Jean-Yves.
  In the shade of a flower : poems (with selected French versions) / by Jean-Yves Solinga. -- 1st ed.
    p. cm.
  Includes glossary.
  Includes index.
  "This is a full length collection of poems ... with French versions of chosen poems. The book is split into three parts: the prologue and epilogue "Multiply Realities," poems in section I "Totems of the Universe," and poems in section II "Droplets of Time."
  ISBN 978-0-9789446-6-7 (pbk. : alk. paper)
  I. Title.
  PS3619.O4326I5 2009
  811'.6--dc22
                        2009032399

Little Red Tree Publishing, LLC
635 Ocean Avenue,
New London, CT 06320
website: www.littleredtree.com

ACKNOWLEDGMENTS

I want to thank once more Michael Linnard of Little Red Tree Publishing for his unfailing professional support and personal friendship beginning with our first book in English *Clair-obscur of the Soul* and its French version *Clair-obscur de l'âme*.

It takes commitment from writers, publishers and readers to keep this art form alive in a world which demands faster and easier communication.

CONTENTS

Foreword by Michael Linnard   viii
Preface by Jean-Yves Solinga   x
Introduction by Jean-Yves Solinga   xii

Prologue: Multiple Realities

Words in Time   1
Fantasies of Proustian Essences   3
Between two languages   5
The Language of Rhinoceroses   6
The anchor-word   7
A market place between two worlds   8
Between the salt weathered rocks and a beach   9
Little voices in our soul: Guilt as art   12
Words written in the dark   12
Doubleganger   13
Dream sequence: Hitting Bottom   16
If nothing else matters… then everything matters   16

Section I - Totems of the Universe

Upon a Funeral Parlor   20
Lying to Oneself   21
Ultimate Philosophical Delusion   23
Haiti: From Barbeque to Misery   24
High School Number   25
Exit the King or Learning How To Die Properly   27
Totems of the Universe   29
* Totems de l'univers   32
First Snow and Big Bang   35
Happy Thoughts   37
Philosophy in a Garage   39
Alexis de Tocqueville, Revisited   40
Ima   42
Girl From a Small New England Town   43
Quilt: All This Wisdom on a Bed   46
View From the Tip of Foreign Policies   47
Emotional Price   49
A Devine Indictment   52
Test of a Contemporary *Job* on Wall Street   53
Memorial Day Fantasy   55
At Least We Were Thin   56
Oncle Jules   57
Chitane   58
* Chitane [originally written in French]   60
Reflections on Olympia by Manet   62
* Réflexions sur l'Olympia de Manet [originally written in French] 63
The Teacher… a Cultivated Nomad   64
The Lascaux Caves   65

To Live in the Moment   66
Don't Look Back   67
Alternate Universe   68
In the Third Person   70
The Keyboard   72

Section II - Droplets of Time

Mimosas   76
* Les mimosas   77
Of Biblical Ancestry and Nude Beaches   78
What Really Counts   79
At Ease With Oneself   80
Beginnings... and the End   81
Reciprocal Visions   83
Manifesto for Gentle Souls   84
The Granite Wall   85
Remembrance of Spring Grass   86
How to Waste Your life   88
Voyage: Making the best of Things   89
Trying to Undo Things   91
* Effort Pour remédier aux choses   93
Emotional Voyeurism   95
* Voyeurisme émotionnel   96
So Close and Yet So Far   97
* Si Proche... et si Loin [originally written in French]   99
Droplets of Time   101
* Gouttelettes du Temps Passé   102
The Taste of Snow   103
Another Life Another Time   104
* Une Autre vie,Une Autre Fois   105
Happiness Made of White   106
* Bonheur Fair de Blanc   107
The Magic Necklace   108
* Le collier magique [originally written in French]   109
Espresso Royal   110
Desert Flower   112
On a Bench   114
* Sur un Banc [originally written in French]   116
Forbidden Fruit   117
* Fruit défendu   119
In the Shade of a Flower   121
* À l'ombre d'une fleur   .123
It Had Been a Long Time Since...   125
* Il y Avait Longtemps... [originally written in French]   127

Epilogue:
Last Glance   129

Glossary   133
Index of Titles and First Lines   137

* A French translation of the preceding poem.

FOREWORD

It is an honor for Little Red Tree Publishing to present Jean-Yves Solinga's third book, *In the Shade of a Flower*, an exceptional collection of poetry. It is not only a wonderful collection of poetry, with select French translations, but it is also supported and contextualized by a prologue and epilogue comprising an extended set of previously unpublished essays called "Multiple Realities." The essays explore Jean-Yves' core intellectual reasoning, beliefs and concepts that underpin this collection and define his philosophy as a writer, poet and artist.

An artist, Jean-Yves asserts, is someone beyond that of a poet or a writer but is one who creates a singularly coherent reality of the "other" outside of the physical reality they themselves inhabit. In many ways a literary transcending experience, beyond the contingent and accidental in the human experience but simultaneously firmly located within their knowledge.

In my experience, it is rare to find a poet so early in his publishing career willing and able to articulate, with such eloquence, precision and style, the motivational reasoning that wills him to write: much less, how and for what purpose, he writes. Jean-Yves takes this opportunity, in his prologue and epilogue, to explain and in the process allows the reader a tantalizing glimpse at that which is behind and beyond the words, the structure, the composition or the syntax of his prosody, into the elemental foundations of his immanent thought processes, which ultimately has its transuent manifestation in the finished poem on the page.

Jean-Yves reaches back into his own immense depth of knowledge and cultural awareness of World, European and French philosophical and artistic literature to reconstruct his own individual "Weltanschauung," an eclectic ideology of what it is, not only, to be a poet, but an artist. He does so in the third person narrative and thus with this dislocation of the narrative voice in fact facilitates an endless range of didactic possibilities and explanations. This carefully assembled ideology is then translated and subsumed into individual poems with such mellifluous grace that it masks and occludes the complexity and technique involved. We are left merely to savor and enjoy the moment created within the poem.

Eschewing more traditional prosodic forms Jean-Yves embraces essentially a free verse or prose style with frequent use of aposiopesises, breaks and groupings of verses creating both a visual and emotional regulator or accelerator to hone each poem's internal dynamic. This is further amplified and compounded by the now familiar multi-layered metaphors, similes, synesthesia and other poetic devises, to which his many followers have become accustomed.

The consistent quality of poetry, as in his previous book *Clair-Obscur of the Soul*, exudes a sense of wonder but in this book they are enhanced by the opening of his own Pandora's Box. At first this exposé may seem to be a moment where a "giving away" of the highly guarded inner secrets of the artist is at hand, like the recipe for a famous drink at long last revealed, but in fact it leaves one in awe of the intellectual journey he has made to arrive at a point of being able to write beautiful poetry that sings and effortlessly falls on the page. They are like that rotating phosphorous light that all artists yearn for in the vastness of the open white page. And we are all richer for knowing and sharing this journey because it is the visible tracks on a literary trodden path: the genesis of an exceptional writer.

In the Shade of a Flower, will live with you for a long time because it is in that delicate metaphorical shade we all at times seek shelter and sanctuary from the maelstrom of our own surd existence. It is also where the unique voice of a truly exceptional existential humanist poet, Jean-Yves Solinga, resides.

Michael Linnard,
New London, Connecticut
August 2009

PREFACE

This is primarily a collection of poems in English but also contains a French version of chosen poems. These are marked in the contents with an asterisk. I have also indicated, in parenthesis, whether the poem was originally written in French. I would add that poems come to me in one or the other language: never in both. Essentially once the idea or the theme of a poem is generally set, I do not even attempt to translate during the writing process. Only when the poem is completely finished in that language do I turn to translating it.

In terms of poetic style, I prefer the freedom of free verse and for poetic effect, I sometimes drop definite, indefinite, possessive articles, etc... to create the cadence of lyrical fluidity. I have also, in one or two places, retained the reverse syntax of the French language for certain phrases as a matter of choice. You will find examples throughout the book.

In general, I would say that in section one "Totems of the Universe" there is a harder edge. It is possibly the reason for my beginning with the images in a funeral parlor.

This part takes its title from a poem of the same name where I examine the "coexistence" of mankind in the midst of an inanimate Universe. One, mankind, is aware, flashy and temporal, the other, stiff, uninterested and usually not interesting [outside of sunrises and sunsets] but seemingly immortal.

By contrast, section two "Droplets of Time" is often more ethereal, introspective. Here again, this section takes its name from one of the poems. Mankind is not going to win the battle against the "formidability" of things; but, in it, we find man grabbing onto the pieces left in the current in order to find some survival, some comfort and hopefully remembrance.

I have learned over time that solace can be found in the intellectual relationship between me and things and their symbolic literary presence. This is in no way a sort of Animism. I am an equal opportunity non believer. But these symbols are the source of my inspiration and a particularly elegant shorthand for imagery.

Hence, my choice for the overall title of this collection: *Under the Shade of a Flower.* In it and under it, I find myself living with the companionship of colors, smells, sounds, shapes, places, pet rooster and magic butterfly that have touched me or were present at pivotal times. In return, I carry them with me always and try to repay them by imprinting the moments on the heart of others. The process of the artistic reconstruction gives predominance to the need for esthetics and therefore biographical details are subservient to that ultimate purpose.

That is exemplified in the painting in the background in my photograph. It was painted by my "Oncle Jules" who was indeed the inspiration for the "Jules" who runs back for the bottle of wine during an Allied bombing raid. Oncle Jules did not die that day. He did, however, paint the Romano-Provençal style Saint Laurent Church of Marseille, destroyed by the Germans. This is how I process the pieces of yesterday.

As for the daily living under the spiritual presence of things past: why not a flower also for me, just like the Little Prince and his rose? Why not relive and reconstruct these moments when, having tried to forget her perfume, she appears again, thanks to that nearby flower, as fresh and as pliable as the first time, as she does in the poem of the same name?

Jean-Yves Solinga
Gales Ferry, Connecticut
July 2009

Jean-Yves Solinga in front of the painting of the Romano-Provençal style Saint Laurent Church of Marseille. (Collection of Jean-Yves)

INTRODUCTION

"Reality does not conform to the ideal, but confirms it."

"All one's inventions are true, you can be sure of that. Poetry is as exact a science as geometry."

Gustave Flaubert

Confronted with the often inescapable frustrating multiple realities of things and others, the seemingly arbitrary societal, political, military injustice and pain, the artist and his art attempt to find some constants in the reconstruction of an awareness of what we call existence.

It is what prompts the artist to make the required effort to transcend space and time and nurture the belief that some "Other," [the observer or reader] will hopefully find some lasting value in the result.

I continue to find poetic prose, as well as poetry's softer and more vaporous sides, to be perfectly suited for the spectrum of images that describe the emotional human condition.

In an idealized setting, reality, harsh reality and poetry would not have to mix. It is instinctively unfair to the universe of both. And yet, mix they do.

The artist deals with both and in his effort to construct imagery and sounds, his art takes nourishment from each. So, in a sometimes complicated breach birth beginning, is born a new world of the imaginary and imagination. It is found at the point of overlap between art for art's sake and the prosaic scene that you have just witnessed in a coffee shop last week.

It happens that digging into the elements of the real, non-fictionalized world can be an unclean process.

Emotional and physical pain, jealousy, abandonment, war and hypocrisy. Fear of the solid, the ephemeral and the everlasting. Fear of what is, should be or can never be. Fear of letting the world enter you and fear of the world ignoring you.

Fear of the next words coming out in a conversation. And fear of hearing nothing evermore.

All these things have often been the source of memorable moments in fiction literature but they make the artist reach into corners of his mind that would be the equivalent of the "dangerous side of the city."

"You don't want to go there: Take my advice!" ...a friendly voice whispers.

And yet, you do go.

This is where life and living are. Not the plastic reproductions of make believe but the acrid smells of carnal presence and memories.

The rich intersection of fiction and nonfiction where the artist shamelessly uses construction equipment as well as very fine screens to reuse or discover anything applicable and convenient.

It is a place where couples break up. Children tragically grow up into adults in five minutes. Where parents drop off their child in the college dorm and know that others will change her now. It is excitement and trepidation that the Father of the Bride feels on his left arm as he walks his daughter to her future.

Where you force yourself to see the one you love with that other: like compulsively picking at a bleeding scab on your shin.

Or finding out once more how much you resent what unpalatable menu death has to offer.

How, in front of the edifice to our humanity – i.e. our intellect – inert totemic symbols, idiotic inorganic things, pick up unrealistic, illusionary, absolute value in an unregulated world that can end in only one conclusion. The gods of Wall Street being just as unforgiving as those of Love and the Old Testament.

The temporal artist compulsively and arrogantly attempts to capture the scenes for immortal posterity. Hopefully in good poetry and with beautiful words. Well turned syntax and explosive matter, antimatter, and/or the antithetical nature of adjectives.

All these things do not change a thing. But maybe, these words can be a road map for the followers. And maybe others will know in a feeling of déjà vu the inexplicable Gothic alchemy of the first glance, the first kiss.

The rest is akin to a smooth Cognac: it helps put a pleasant tone to inevitable finality.

It is better than silence. And that should be good.

Jean-Yves Solinga
Gales Ferry, Connecticut
July 2009

PROLOGUE

MULTIPLE REALITIES

What follows is a collection of short essays, using an unnamed third person narrative to facilitate a greater literary range and freedom, which essentially delineates various concepts and ideas I have used in my poetry. Below each section title I have referenced an example poem from this book where I have applied that particular concept or idea.

WORDS, IN TIME
(e.g. Remembrance of Spring Grass, page 86)

He had decided long ago that in the brotherhood of the unfaithful, for those who cannot themselves let go, that there can only be belief in the solidity and seriousness of things anchored in the temporal and material realities.

For these serious people, Santa Claus is too much fraught with gratuitous joy.

They have entered the world of adults. Not unlike the experiences of the Little Prince as he leaves his rose behind to travel to the planets.

And then, he thought to himself, there are those for whom happiness requires only a coat of snow and the sound of parents downstairs in the corner kitchen to set their heart at ease and make them certain that all is well and that tomorrow will be the same as today. That somewhere it is written that bad things only happen, or should happen, to the guy who kicks dogs or kills political malcontents.

He had left the world of the innocence of youth and had become aware that there were individuals who upon exiting the doors of religious establishments, on their individual Sabbath day, would blindly follow the precepts of hate, doubt and emotional discrimination as they go back to the office. And these same believers, in only the solid things of hard currency, thick walls of protection, gated lives and clear diamonds, would kill and die for the simple colors of the cloth of flags, the particularly weird behavior of the Other and the particular historical syntax of dusty religious books.

It happens, in the meantime, that in some other people, in some parts of their lives, magic does happen. Needs to happen.

That Merlin, the enchanter, can appear from behind a rock formation, and offer to some of us, lucky enough, a drink of that potion.

1

That is when he felt the need to write a story. An hallucinatory tale, a wishful list, which one could enter at any point and take part in, and find something relevant.

Such as palpable beauty, solid memories, the immediacy of a presence or a moment. At times exquisitely precious. At times painfully gone.

A Christmas list for adults to fill the empty half of our lives. The half in need or searching for the impossible: a return to time irrevocably gone.

That of the "first time," which some of us spend the rest of our lives reconstructing with pieces of words: thus hopefully forming a mosaic of passion.

That time when you go around the car to say good night and she does not move away. She just stands there and all the veneer of proper decorum has been stripped away and all that is left is the obsession of the roundness of lips and her breath taking hug.

And so, at the crossroad of love and art, we enter the temple of Baudelaire. A temple built where is found the need and the means to give form and continuity to some transparent and vaporous "truths." These truths speak about the conscience of a concept of the beautiful that is facing an unfortunate eternal void between extremes: between now, lunch and death.

We sneak into a Holy of Holies where religious artifacts and references give support to antithetical contrasts between the attraction of the fleshy amoral and the need for the appearance, at least, of the immortal.

During hours of writing, his dog, had remained religiously at his feet. Never giving him the impression that she needed to stop Time in Time to wag her tail out of happiness.

Later, a few days after her death, the remnants of her "deeds" were still to be seen in the yard. These little mounds were more and more petrified by the sun and destroyed by the rain and had become an obsession for him. He found himself seeing more spirituality in this fecal presence that in the smart alcohol-fed repartees of social evenings.

There was a difficult iconic truth in front of what was left of this animal: the need, the obsession to somehow leave Time behind or outside of him and keep the best of it to replay at his pleasure.

If it was so for his dog then he could do it for his mother's glance or her glance. Anyone. A summer butterfly, maybe.

"You need," he thought to himself, "only to not let reality interfere."

The secret, he assumed, was to go through that stage and not let the present re-invade his thoughts. To not go back to the more ambivalently pressing: such as work on a obligatory power point presentation or the pile of dishes.

"The secret is in what André Gide wrote. To let yourself be available."

This is, indeed, what he was looking for. What he discovered. His own Proustian Madeleine while driving on a dark highway.

He liked the illusion in his mind that art, in its more generous personal short term and longer term definitions, is a Time Machine that would allow him to vanquish, to mock and to disdain Time itself.

Art and words were his tools that liberated him from Things, from Matter and in so doing, linked him outside of this Matter to the Other.

To this little beach of his youth.

Words, until science comes up with something better, would allow him to live, to relive the past. That is their magic, their strength and in particular the price that they demand of us.

Because some of these memories can, at times, be neither kind nor moral. And many times selfish and self serving.

But, thanks to them, he could believe in the ability to live in two universes at the same time: a multiplicity of realities. One, in a reality that is physical and full of the glue of the present and the other of his choice: artistic, multiple and based on his needs, without divine references and out of the social and human norms.

He had carried images, faces and smells in his soul all this time. The sights, smells and sensations that he had never been able to classify and put away on some shelf because they had refused to make a whole.

They always seemed to have a crack in them: between light and darkness. He felt as though he had carried within him a clair-obscur, a chiaroscuro of the soul.

With events and relationships resolved in time and space, he was left with only art as a means to create a parallel world with reflections in that voyeuristic mirror that had been witness to important moments in his life.

His thoughts returned to his university days. To his introduction to the character of Caligula in the play of the same name by Albert Camus. Here was a man, Caesar of Rome, who had imposed no less than the personal intimate and sensual acquisition of the moon as a standard for his own happiness.

"All I want," he thought to himself, "is to put her back in my arms. How difficult could that be compared to what Caligula wanted?"

FANTASIES OF PROUSTIAN ESSENCES
(e.g. Totems of the Universe, page 29)

His fingers, in the meantime, had been clenched on the steering wheel of his car. He was closely watching the moving shadows that seemed to jump to life behind every bush hit by the headlights.

He didn't know what to make of the evening.

"There is such a thing as too much information to process."

"I can't make any sense of things."

At one more of his academic functions, he had been introduced to a professional woman. As un-sexy as it sounded, it was her knowledge of international politics that excited him. Her travels as an international lawyer had taken her everywhere... twice. She seemed to have absorbed any language and culture with which she came into contact. And to make her even more formidable in his eyes: she had added all types of cooking styles to her repertoire. He could hear himself make that sexist comment that did not impress or insult those who knew him:

"That's what you get for letting women vote."

Further mumbling: "How can she know more than I do?"

And then there was the issue of the medical coverage in Western Europe.

"I can't stand it. I actually asked her about that! She must think that my idea of breaking the ice of awkward moments must be to ask about such things as "existentialism.""

"Come to think about it... it is."

"I'm sure she's thrilled with all of this!"

In her, cohabited the analytical mind of a lawyer. And a deep "virile femininity," one of his favorite concepts.

Versus his own impressionistic view of people, learning and living. A shot gun approach to logic and wisdom. An uncanny borderline irresponsibility for making reality co-exist with literature.

It made for multifaceted sexual tension.

He loved it!

The radio was off. As was the case when he tried to concentrate on the driving. This is when he unknowingly brushed his right index by his nostrils.

The steering of the car had now lost his interest. And while he was driving too fast for the conditions, late at night and in absolute blackness except for a beam of white on the road, his mind was instead on the skin laid bare on the back of her cocktail dress.

He thought that he had both his driving and the conduct of his life well in hand. A tenured university position, sabbaticals to travel, adulatory peer respect and an endless renewed stream of social "activities."

When the apparently accidental sniffing of his fingers brought him back to the dance floor and her presence.

The hypnotic flashes of forms going by the side of the road in the periphery of his sight sent him back to the trembling embrace still warm on his chest. What made the moment even more precious was its unexpected prompting. It was as though his body wanted to remind him, in spite of him, without him, outside of him, of her perfume, of her smell...

Recurrent with him, he had a non-linear time event. His mind starter to wander outside of this car... this night.

BETWEEN TWO LANGUAGES
(e.g. Alexis de Tocqueville: Revisited, page 40)

He had done what any good immigrant was supposed to do. He had soaked up American culture. The process was made that much more natural and pleasurable by the fact that it took place over his teenage years.

Time went by and with the death of his parents he had fewer reasons and opportunities to use his mother tongue. It seemed that his past, which had been so much associated with the joys and depth of his culture... this past had been slowly drying up in his veins.

All these thoughts were going through his mind. He was on the same road of his previous long trips, years before, when he was finishing a doctorate. A doctorate whose very existence, he thought, would help him preserve his idealized past hours on this little beach in Morocco.

A little beach called Sidi Moussa.

And thus he ended up spending hours on the snowy roads of New England to write a thesis in a French language that had been marginalized by the military defeats of History.

"History," he had convinced himself, based on his cultural susceptibilities and his reading of political science texts, "is written by these victors."

Later on, after hours in the now artificial neon lights, he felt the impulse to write poetry about his organic solar youth, knowing that anything in his mother tongue would have to be read through the filtered flavor of the wooden osmosis of translation.

Incongruously, driving through this Rockwellian setting of snowy New England roads, his mind turned to another textbook illustration, this one of his elementary school days.

It was that of a victorious Julius Caesar sitting on a resplendent throne after the Gallic Wars facing the haughty defeated leader of the Gauls, Vercingetorix, at his feet surrounded by Roman swords and symbols.

It occurred to him, in turn, that he, also would not easily give up his language, his culture.

And that, although, in an ever global and technically dependent world, he did not see a happy ending, he would offer himself a moment of fantasy by seeing a similarity in the Gaul chieftain facing the unstoppable Roman invasion.

Just like this Gaul, there was futile pride in his heart in front of the Anglophone onslaught. Nevertheless, he pictured him breathing into his lungs the last fresh air of the still virginal woods of Burgundy full of the smells of roasting wild boars and honey based beer.

This was taking place far from the smart technical constructions and edifices of the Roman Empire. He could therefore not hear or feel behind him its rigid conformism through the thickness of his disdain. He was blind as to the enormous danger of the latent imposition of the homogenization, in the next few generations, that were about to stifle him and his people.

He liked to think, therefore, that this is the same disdain that the Roman soldier saw in the eyes of the blond be-speckled neck of the "imperious" and impassible prisoner just before the blade touched it.

That Roman soldier, that night, must have returned home wondering why this primitive Gaul could not have accepted the logic of the strength of the movement of which his blade was the clear, straight and personal extension.

THE LANGUAGE OF RHINOCEROSES
(e.g. Ultimate Philosophical Delusion, page 23)

He felt like the protagonist in Ionesco's play, *Rhinocéros*. Bérenger, the last human being, remains surrounded by these enormous beasts with distant eyes. They know and care nothing of his past. The very poetic beauty and elasticity of his mother tongue escapes them.

He had kept, next to him, as he composed in French, a dictionary from his father's army days. It was held together by tape: a proper metaphor for his cultural decrepitude.

He was like one these sailors left for years alone on an island with, as sole companion, a text that he had grabbed, by chance and at random, just before going overboard. In this dusty text would have existed all that he would remember of his language as he tried to engage the curious birds of the island into a dialog.

Driving in the mortal cold of this New England night, he felt the presence of the warmth of the North African sirocco on the nape of his neck.

It was you, Sidi Moussa calling him back to the substances in the past that make up the contrasting pieces of mosaic of what he was.

Sharp edged and of varied origins, these little stones had come together, as best as possible. The finished product of this mural was a declaration, an enumeration of things that had become important to him. And just like these mosaics of representations of daily chores and ever present lust on Roman villas' walls, they will easily outlast its owners and capture the attention of the future passerby and hopefully, gently, find echoes in this Other's glance.

THE ANCHOR-WORD
(e.g. Espresso Royal, page 110)

It is in the very sound of your name, Sidi Moussa, that he attempted to remake things. The very solidity of the "anchor-word" that would return him to what counted. To visions that had been drowned by the waves of Time and, yet, that he had preciously kept in a waterproof pouch made of passion.

Time: the mortal enemy that effaces so easily the memories of the glance and the heart.

Sidi Moussa, you are the souvenir-link, the nomenclature that stood up to the temporal whiteness that threatened passion.

Passion, whose mortal enemy is the absence of the pastels found in the nuances of one's life.

This drabness of life made up of moments like staying a little longer at work. Whereupon we find out afterward that we have missed the visit of an ex-best friend who had stopped unexpectedly at the house after years of silence. We are left instead with our drink in our hand on the back porch, alone, trying to reconstruct these memories that were rekindled by the very value of what this name had always meant in our life.

It is upon looking nonchalantly over the familiar bundle of flowers around the patio that we realize how surprisingly close to our consciousness were these moments all this time, had we taken the time to whisper its symbols under our breath.

Like the snows of the Labrador, Time freezes the trembling sensations of the moment until an eternal cosmic cold replaces, by its dumb presence, the fragile pulsating human glance.

"Sidi Moussa, you are the phoneme that is the last and only link to things that can be more real than the page upon which I am talking to you," he whispered.

Not unlike the breathlessness that follows the first musical notes of a song that puts you back, as we drive to work, back at a university football game against Yale, with her presence. That sensation that gives you tunnel vision, such was her importance, amid the animal house atmosphere.

And then, you are sitting at a red light, in the middle of traffic thirty years later and "it is all there," the music, the intimate conversation in the frantic football stadium, the side-glance... all these pieces of our past exist in these bundles of stimuli.

All that is required sometimes is the fervor, the enunciation of things that have disappeared in Time. Sometimes the simple denotation of precious names and impulses is all that is needed to produce the sorcery of the magic of litanies that bring back temporarily forgotten places and people...

"Sidi Moussa. Sidi Moussa."

A MARKET PLACE BETWEEN TWO WORLDS
(e.g. Emotional Voyeurism, page 95)

As an adult, few things split his soul more than the innate, instinctive realization that he had felt like an intruder in his own past. He had spent his youth in the abundant wealth of two cultures: European and Maghreban. He thought in particular about the colonial market frequented by his parents. Its white-washed walls protected the building from the intrusive heat of the sun. Baffled windows running along the top brought in some fresh air like pockets of rarified oxygen. While at the very doors of the market co-existed the dual and indeed multiple natures of the reality of this site. Outside, were the tempting smells of contradictory products being cooked on dangerously perched fryers and the sweet-acrid smell of leather goods sold just a few feet from expensive Belgium chocolate and forbidden pork products.

The visions in this place should have been shocking to a European youngster. But later on in life, he had accepted these as powerful and living metaphors for what, in proper circles, we call the hidden symbols of nascent sensuality.

At the back of the market, an emanation of the smell of urine and manure from the horses and donkeys grabbed his throat. And yet, he could not understand why the pounding of these smells provoked an irresistible pleasure in him.

There was a contradictory gentleness that was spinning around the brutality of these continually beaten animals. A peaceful resignation reigned over all this injustice and proliferation of things and colors. Gigantic flies fed over this entire hellish table. And to his surprise: everything seemed "good!" A sort of convenient dispensation from the canon of his catechism had been ordained making the spectacle suitable for a little boy.

As he waited for his parents inside the solid protection of the car, his passive and helpless presence put him, and all the accoutrements of his "civilizing" culture and tastes, in his "place" amid things: he was a voyeur. A resignation took over him between revolt, disgust and pleasure. He felt ambivalence between what should have been and what pleased him.

The danger he had learned in retrospect that day is, that what pleases us, shamefully and too often, appears quite simply in front of us.

Fortunately, amid the emotional chaos of the cinéma-vérité of this setting, he knew that he had the still reliable presence of a maternal presence that would always protect him. Not unlike his belief in Santa Claus. But, while holding on to this maternal hand, he felt the duality of things opening up in front of him: One was, by definition clean and innocent, and the other, according to his body, cruel and sensual. This duality exemplified the complex nature of happiness. It would feed and fill his corporal intimacy and would define, better than most of his learned textbooks, his unease as to its source when facing future ecstasy.

BETWEEN THE SALT WEATHERED ROCKS AND A BEACH
(e.g. So Close and Yet So Far, page 97)

He was back in his youth. It is a place between the cliffs and the ocean. In it, a minuscule beach exists within a space filled with possibilities.

He felt this past unfold directly on the other side of the windshield. An uncontrollable urge made him reconstruct and address this pivotal moment.

"Sidi Moussa, my friend, this secular beach is within sight of your religious monument. I can still see a promontory of cliffs covered with little holes in the fashion of bees nests."

Indeed, the sea salt had weaved a fragile mineral lace. One would have thought that the simple act of stepping over it would have flattened the stone fabric itself. And yet, these cliffs were as solid as their earthly mothers. They had forgotten none of their rocky ancestry. They had only lost the appearance of solidity.

In order to reach the little beach, it was necessary to deal with the natural trompe l'oeil of the landscape. The very strength of the substance was hidden under the attractive gentleness of Things. A constant backdrop of intoxicating noise from the bitter green waves of the Atlantic added a disconcerting stimulus to the senses.

He remembered feeling completely weak–kneed as he reached the bottom of the cliffs. The moon shaped beach was made of hard grayish sand. Nature had done its best to jealously surround the site and protect it from prying and envious eyes.

The moment and the landscape became intertwined in the privileged richness of the glance upon Things that were opening up.

The young man, had never experienced this sugary astonishment of sight. Trembling, he was starting to realize that he could possess what he saw... to possess one's glance!

He had found his way to this beach along and alone with his long time family friend: a girl slightly older than he was.

An inkling of subliminal corporal intimacy was symbolized by their bathing suits. All this was taking place away from the ever present, often reproachful maternal glance.

For what seemed the first time, he felt an essential link with the outside world. A feeling of "availability" not only from himself toward this world but a reciprocal flow.

And yet, he had previously had this general envy vis-à-vis Things. He had, for instance, found that this girl's multi-color hazel eyes reminded him of his prize marble. He also liked her collection of toy sport cars: but they were hers and she would not share!

The experience, well before he knew how to intellectualize it, was a prise de conscience that was akin to a fever. It was trying to tell him that he could try to completely, physically take hold of the totality of what he coveted. That place, later in life, when and where he would realize that he could leave molecules of himself behind and thus contemplate extending and propagating into Time and Space.

He would conclude years later that it was not even the act itself that counted but rather the importance of its very existence among other possibilities that would confront him in the future.

Because, ultimately, he did panic in front of what he was seeing and refused.

But, to see and to understand the beauty, the majesty!

It was giving him access to the closest thing to eternity. This fact would stay with him as he later tried to hang on to shreds of beliefs when all other ones had failed him.

He whispered to himself, at that mundane stop light:

"This must be why things are at times disarmingly gentle in spite of their apparent harshness."

"Sidi Moussa, you were a witness next to me at this moment when nubile sensuality offered itself to me. Yet I looked away. The truth sometimes is scary."

"I did turn away. I turned toward the wild winds blowing at the top of your sandy beach."

"I turned toward temporary childhood tranquility waiting at the top of the cliff: dependable companionship of maternal protection that was meant to ultimately and tearfully go away."

But he knew, henceforth, that in spite and amidst the confusion and quieting of his still pounding heart that a measure of himself could impose itself, even if temporarily, on the World.

"The rocks had the color of her skin, he sighted to himself."

"And your cliffs, Sidi Moussa, had fixed this event in the solidity of our glance."

The microcosm of this setting contained the glory of a rite of passage forever repeated. The little boy and the young girl have disappeared and so has their innocence.

He wondered what had happened to Sidi Moussa.

He had long ago decreed that Sidi Moussa was and would remain alive and beautiful. And that is what counted.

Then, he heard rumors of its death. Death by the neglect of the living. People who did not know its worth. They were too promiscuously close to it. People, busily living around it, in the blindness of their daily lives, had turned it into a garbage dump.

Like a fisherman who curses the dangerous sharp rocks of an otherwise beautiful port entrance.

"Why not incase them in a cement jetty and be done with this threat to shipping?"

"Wouldn't your isolated pretty beach, Sidi Moussa, make an ideal refuse dump?"

Well! That is what he had heard about you. Your "death" amid oily papers and rats. With flying plastic bags and dirt.

He was devastated.

He did not know how to stop time for you.

You see, the gods, have their own immortality, which we humans have given to them. While your site, Sidi Moussa, is much more fragile and was linked apparently to the shivers of his molecules.

He had thought all this time that your solidity had been made absolute by the presence of the Marabout nearby in whose hands he had left you.

In the meantime you had become the intermediary through which he would come back to the sweet waters and dreams after his own messianic voyages. For he knew that between the endless desert wanderings and the final rest under the date trees existed his inevitable death.

But some deaths simply leave us red eyed and glancing upon our expected loss. But there are deaths that stop everything in the fullness of life and leave us with nothing before or after.

Upon hearing of your death he declared:

"Let it be said and let it be written that your little white beach is unapproachably precious and forever perfect."

The Troubadours would sing a Send Off at the conclusion of their declamations: often invoking the protection of the also inapproachable Virgin Mary.

He thought of a more carnal and pagan version:

"May the sensuality of her glance be your protector saint, Sidi

Moussa."

"May she be as affectionate to you as she was to me."

"And may it be that everything, that is humanly beautiful, lives in an ephemeral mortal moment of happiness under your maghrebin sun."

LITTLE VOICES IN OUR SOUL: GUILT AS ART
(e.g. The Granite Wall, page 85)

Over the mechanical whining of the tires he heard them, these same voices. He would hear them again and again when he least expected them.

He solemnly surveyed his conscience. He would have heard them even if he had been determining the purchase of a new shirt.

They interfered with mighty or meaningless things.

He had thought that the weights and counter-weights of Good and Evil had been put away. But here they were again: making him swear not to repeat his deeds:

"Let her be... you have done enough hurt!" He could hear in the dark.

Then images of temptation would unfold in front of him. He would outstretch his hands towards the sweets like the little boy that he was often accused of remaining.

All the philosophical infrastructures, all the academic lectures, all the wisdom of encyclopedias would try to rush to his aid.

The cold analysis of Sartre was replaced by the warmth of Camus. The quasi-Puritanism of Pascal replaced by the escapism of Rimbaud as well as the bad conscience of Baudelaire, prisoner in the arms of Parisian hedonism.

As penitence, he would express, in the first person singular, concepts like: immortality, freedom of action, the impossibility of not being free; and actions that commit us inescapably to our future.

At the university dinner table he would hear from his colleagues about family consequences and societal rules, while his own little voices would stay quiet.

"There is no guidance to go along with dessert," he could hear. Not sure if that came from his friends or himself.

Temptation was at home in his soul: sitting in its favorite easy chair. Evil and the easy way, he found out and in spite of his existential stance, had not been chased away: they had never been.

In fact, he heard voices giving him easily reachable hope for the last instants of his mortal life.

Between Good and Evil, he was faced with the cream colored

translucent pearls and the richness of shadowy existence. These pearls were all ambivalently available.

This is when he repeated words and warning from his Catechism days: "Upon your death: what will you feel?"

"Will you ask yourself if you did the right things?"

"Will you have any regrets?"

The atheist that he had become would wake up in front of his conscience and in the sweat of a moist pillow. He heard the mechanism of the watch on his forearm.

He could feel a warm wetness at the corner of his eyes as he tried to fall back to sleep in what was left of his life and the driveway to shovel in the morning darkness.

WORDS WRITTEN IN THE DARK
(e.g. Philosophy in a Garage, page 39)

The last few preceding days had gone the way society learns to impose them on humanity. That is, worried about tight schedules and missed taxis. Oblique glances from co-workers and intrusive questions from close friends or family members.

Ignored sunsets over New York city. Long profile of the slender Long Island white beaches from his favorite left window of the commuting plane to Boston.

Then waking up in their own apartments with obligatory stacks of legal briefs and literary essays spread on their respective half empty beds.

She had no idea that her law degree came with this sad imposition on her private life: complicated voids. That's a disclaimer that she had missed.

And he, who would lecture all semester long about the ideals of ideas. The effervescence of happiness from inspired syntax and brush strokes. Visions on the human scale of immortal happiness in clever reconstructions of human dreams.

And, here he was, damning every line of his students' dreams that he had to correct. Impersonal professorial time that took him away from replaying in his mind their intimate conversations.

DOUBLEGANGER
(e.g. In the Third Person, page 70)

He couldn't fall back to sleep. He replicated the pivotal scene on the darkness of his bedroom wall.

His mind was vividly watching moments of his life that seemed to be regurgitating the bile of existential guilt.

There was something formally sad in her glance. It was something that he had rarely seen in her.

She seemed to take a deep breath as though she had stopped breathing since they had walked in from the kitchen. There was silence. As though imposed from a higher authority. An invisible judge ready to pass sentence.

He remembered that he didn't have the energy to break the inertia. The judgment, any judgment, had to come from her. Unsoiled by him.

She said:

"All I ever needed from you, was you." That's what I saw and loved.

"I knew about the strings of your profession and your habits."

"And I didn't care."

"But now, that is all that I see. These strings that bring you back to your way of life."

"To these material things and people that defined and still define you."

"Your diplomas. Your publications. You professional circuits."

"All that I ever wanted has remained at the level of a dream."

"It is still a dream and I don't want to turn it into a nightmare."

"I don't want it to have a life of its own."

"I want to own this dream as it was."

"But for that, I must free myself."

"I must know that I can count on those close to me to be good to me and my self-worth."

"I must be able to trust those with whom I am susceptible, to know that I am susceptible."

"Not to take advantage of me... how you, in the final analysis took advantage of me and gave nothing in return."

This thought flashed in his mind:

"She can't be talking about me! I'm not that person!"

She continued:

"I was alone and naked in this place where my conscience was flying around me like a crazed spirit and was taunting me with my own words of wisdom."

"Words of my past."

"Of a past made of what I thought was integrity and strength."

"...My integrity and strength..." she repeated in a barely audible whisper.

She had finished these words as she was looking away. When she turned back, he fully expected to see tears in her eyes.

Nothing!

Her eyes were stone dry! Her glance had the intensity, the clear simplicity of intelligence... yes, intelligence.

As though she was defending a thesis. Merciless. Almost inhuman.

Academic.

She continued.

"You had, or rather, I accused you of ripping me away from all that was good."

"I could not allow you or your image in my heart to become so evil and dirty."

"I decided that we had to go our separated way."

"Do you understand? "

He had listened to every word of this speech as though his very life had been in the balance of the very bundling of words, the sequence and syntax and the use of a particular vocabulary. The next verb and adjective.

He was amazed and disgusted. It was like watching a movie with a good script.

He caught himself thinking that he wished he could have written the same thing. It was as though he was proofreading a student essay on "the great love of my high school life."

It occurred to him that artists must go through life plagiarizing these moments. Mining the anguish around them for nuggets of imagery and inspiration.

The caring and honorable person that he believed he was made him ashamed at the joy of the artist that was taking mental notes. Ashamed to be alive in front of this dying soul.

He was violating this very intimate moment for future use.

It was what was nagging him that he was taking pointers for how he would better fit these words and thoughts in his next play.

It was mental rape. And like a repeat offender he could not help himself again. She was handing him all this beautiful material.

Instead of feeling guilt and looking away from her beautiful, still beautiful glance, he was instead drawing as much power, as much passion out of those words and eyes.

Like many writers before and many still after, he heard this Machiavellian voice in his head:

"At least, some good is going to come out of all this! "

And that is when it happened. For the first – seriously the first time ever – he thought that the only way to deal with his deeds, with the consequences of his actions, was to destroy his work:

"It is not her image or the inspiration that counts."

"This is what some artists must have come to realize in the past."

"So that must be why some artists destroy their work," he thought…

…he closed his eyes.

DREAM SEQUENCE: HITTING BOTTOM
(e.g. Lying To Oneself, page 21)

And so, he now had to find inspiration at a time that it had become just a cursor on the flatness of a blue screen. It was not the first time that he had faced this type of artistic nihilism. It is a time when he would look for the essence of feelings cooked up in the bowels of personal hell. Finding himself scrapping the dry residues of yesterday. He would lick them like some block of bitter salt on the part of a thirsty cow back from the pasture.

What an image! Looking for an inspirational muse under the guise of this white dry powder that bites into your tongue.

An then... An acidic sensation! It would transport him again. He would put down his glass of Beaujolais and start listening to this evil, destructive bubbling inside of him...

This dried up essence was the most concentrated and pernicious that he had ever felt to this point.

It is all over. There is no remaining reason to write.

"I would rather walk mindlessly the streets than put another thought on paper."

And yet, what would wash over his mind was like what they call in classical cooking: une réduction.

It is the best of a veal bouillon reduced to its very essential ingredients. The sort of intensity of taste that goes beyond the moment. It stays, it enters your memory bank. The kind of taste that you can reconstruct, at will later, on your palate.

That is when you instinctively know that the cosmological and emotional void you feel at that instant will produce some of the best passages.

IF NOTHING ELSE MATTERS... THEN EVERYTHING MATTERS
(e.g. What Really Counts, page 79)

The slightest pieces of the past and future are all that matters. Like *Job* in front of his god, he felt naked and without pretension. His very pores were communicating with things.

Like the humble prophet, he had become an empty vessel ready to accept the magic mash of the dirt of the world. The very stuff that will ferment into what makes it worthwhile for you to be the only thing between an amoebae and the stellar grandness: a thinking thing.

And in spite of his doubts about the exact literary position of the narrative-narrator void or closeness. In spite of the exact position on man and mankind in the spectrum that spans the nausea of the solid world and the exaltation of religious revelation, he knew deep down that what he had to say was better than saying nothing.

She was gone and so were the days of the immediacy in his arms of touching this object of desire followed by the immediacy of explosions of images and words to capture the moment.

So he decided to transfer these moments, these words, to the blackboard of the future and let the world in on it.

It is now morning, in a hotel room in some Asian capital, he has noticed a streak of four or five really white hairs on his previously jet black forehead. Not gray: but white. And all he could think about was blackness. The one of his black pompadour of adolescence and that of the boyish black hair style of a woman in Paris.

He had mechanically made a cup of coffee, which minutes latter appeared in his left hand. He had not wanted to drink coffee this early in the morning. But here it was. This cup of coffee seemed stupidly, inertly, to contain all the basic truth of his life at that moment.

Materiality seem to have more importance and purpose than his own will and determination as whether to chose driving to work or grabbing his passports… all three of them.

Of doing the right thing over fantasy. Or the other way around.

Upon taking his first drops of this coffee he was swallowing the same wisdom based bitterness of childhood medicine.

This coffee was invading his bowels with all the contradictions that dying dreams of eternal youth have in front of inevitable and immortal awareness of oblivion.

This coffee was an intrusion through the automatic replication of the act which allowed the mind to be cleared for other reflections.

That warm liquid had a very existence outside of his will and desire. And it would enter his body and would become cold. Seemingly like his life if not his thoughts.

She was gone. It was over. All the clichés that you want. But that cup of coffee said it all. Efficiently and unsparingly.

He opened his laptop and began writing.

At the lowest and most longing.

At the very worst and very best to paraphrase an important opening of literature. With all these images to follow.

Like a dying man in the desert, he looked around and knew that every single scrap of thought that he could put together in his notebook was his best offering for that anonymous future Other.

Because these words will have been filtered through the coals of conviction and authenticity.

And that the formers are the last existing link to human beauty and memory.

Flower of paradise in the window over looking the church of Saint Germain-des-Prés in Paris, drawn by Katy Norman.

PART I

TOTEMS OF THE UNIVERSE

UPON A FUNERAL PARLOR

Where everything will end,
He can conceive of a future in his absence.
Others will dutifully take part without him.

Having often kept track of the number of cars
Of preceding funeral processions.

Murmuring:
"How many, in turn, will I have?"

He will be quietly envious of the living.
These men accompanied by elegant women.

In black body hugging dresses
Usable for both… funerals and cocktail parties.

"Will I have the same audience?"
"Will they be there for me?"

This might just be the ultimate Faustian bargain:
To be a member of one's own funeral reception line.

Breathing in… no, swallowing
In a last hedonistic act,

The expensive perfumes
Evaporating from overheated feminine flesh.

Reflection upon the 'reception line' at a funeral parlor.

LYING TO ONESELF

It takes religious courage for love
To face its antithesis.

The death of itself in front
Of the darkness of abnegation.

The force fed atheism of love:
Like a hapless Galileo in his moldy cell.

Turning one's back on celestial truths.
And then, to carry within you, the stigmata of your beliefs
Etched on the pupil of your soul.

The great inquisition of the heart is opened
For all of society to see. In order to set it at ease.

Forced to forget what was so dear,
So necessary... to define the day at its sunrise.

We are led to the new Holy of Holies
Only to find, walking up the granite steps of eternity,

Remnants of the hours of the hedonism of secular splendor
And the hissing sound of still warm and golden relics.

Unreligious steamy images of an ecstatic smile.
Vapors of intimacy in the clouds of humanistic incense.

The omnipresence of her godlike glance
From atop the peristyle of stone.

Then the ultimate stipulated denial and betrayal.
Letting oneself go into the darkness,
To avoid saying the words.

The ultimate defeat... the one that dries
The lush landscape of Paradise
Of all possible streams of happiness.

Paying the ultimate price in pounds of flesh:

In the currency of taking away the right to hear her name.

And to convince oneself that it now carries
The heretic smells of old religion.

Living, now, in forced agnosticism.
The ultimate fear... that of tomorrow.

Days now void of a presence and a touch.
A solitary room now taking on
The limitless dimensions of space and time.

She is on the other side of this universe
And no wormhole to reach it.

A place where molecules lose their warmth
And frigidity stalks humanity.

In this void, the inevitable asphyxia of love sets in.
We do the proper thing. We get on our knees

And solemnly proclaim out loud the imposed credo:

That things... in which we believed...
...are not true... and will never be.

Atheism of Love

ULTIMATE PHILOSOPHICAL DELUSION

Flowing sacramental robes of precious silk.

Phalanges of followers and rumors of unseen accomplishments.
Strictly choreographed appearances and oratories.

Rituals of all sorts and colors. Rules with self serving regulations.
Laws with built-in prejudices of attitudes and conformities.

Encrusted with the stifling legal mud of precedent setting dirt
That makes heretical any fundamental changes.

Like a national casino,
The house eventually will win.

Military and political leaders
Define themselves by the Other's glance.

It is the ultimate dishonest Existential dialog.
"I am what you say I am."

With adoring looks, with fearful looks,
With confused looks upon their status,

Authorities thus gather their authority
Making mere humans born of mere humans

Somehow less organically based, and at times,
Magically produced or inspired

With irrefutable and unquestionable wisdom
That we wrap in a self-imposed crap shoot,

Hoping that we chose well our religious and political shepherds
Until we rise up and install a comparable institution.

Lord of the Flies revisited. Sometimes, a pig is just a pig

HAITI: FROM BARBEQUE TO MISERY

You have to be proud of mankind
Since it left its cave for a better one.

Its wooden hut for its neighbor's.
Its culture for the stolen jewels of others.

Ah! Darwin… what a man!

He made it possible to blame the inevitable:
"It's not me… it's my DNA."

So this flashes by my mind
As a documentary on Barbeque goes scientifically by.

For it proclaimed that some of the earliest examples
Of this backyard cooking was seen on that island.

Quasi naked people frolicking around the smoke
Of the juicy local animal fauna on wooden trestles.

Unnaturally happy in their natural ways.
Oblivious as to their lack of European bliss and undergarments.

As images of the present setting nag me:
Deforested lunar landscape.

The poorest of poorest descendants of African slaves.
And the fumes escaping from burning dumps,

As today's plat du jour.

Upon watching a culinary documentary on the history of Barbeque, hoping a future reader finds a different ending.

HIGH SCHOOL NUMBER

Young couple on the uneven urban sidewalk.
Concrete surface splintered and disintegrated by the winter's cold.

Both the cement and their faces aged beyond their years
Downstream from societal, educational and emotional neglect.

Surroundings of shards of wine bottles.
Burnt out neon signs and vain screams of car alarms.

Young child in tow well beyond bed time.
Tired girlfriend at a respectful regal two steps behind.

Obligatory beer can in hand and a generous wave
To all his friends against the wall of boredom.

Parade of destitution
Down this main street of too many anywheres USA

Like the returning astronauts of yesterday
In the canyons of celebrity
But, he... has never broken the gravity of soiled grounds.

His jeans and multicolored snickers
Well stuck to the flattened gum on empty parking lots.

Mother... Mother what has happened to your children?

His football player bulk
Was no protection from the tackles of destiny

His slim physique and talent
Have been integrated in the mud of a distant sports field

He turns left into a dead end alley of his present life
As the sodium street lights reflect

On the cracking plastic letters of a State Football Championship
Glued to fading High School chemical colors.

That now stand as the artificial essence

Of his momentary happiness.

Mother, Mother... what has happened to your children?

Walking in an urban setting years after the dream.
To the sound of Marvin Gaye's "What's happening brother?"

EXIT THE KING OR LEARNING HOW TO DIE PROPERLY

Personal, intimate horizons becoming more and more limited.
Our thoughts, our hopes… shamelessly restricting themselves
To the lumps and creases of our bed sheets…

…Instead of the flat stones on the Baie des Anges of Nice.

When limited time is limited
To the next application of a wet towel on our lips
Instead of the firmness of her lips against a sunbathed kiss.

When the vanishing totems of life
Vaporize themselves to the token sterile medical presence
Of a semi anonymous face and fingers on the pulse of our wrist.

When yesterday's platitude and boredom of food shopping
Takes on the now escaping value
Of precious memories of once walking freely down the aisles.

Our glance… amazed by the encroaching stillness of things
Mimicking our own.

We observe from our increasingly stationary place
Visions of the various possessions of our lives.

The carnal, molecular and moist ones.
Even the plasticized, homogenized, artificial ones,

Those of the mind and of the heart,
All of them radiant and valuable.

All these Things… had been with us all along
In our part of the dusty cosmos.
Faithful exciting companions in an otherwise dead universe.

In the augmenting immobility…
…Sounds of a significant sensual laughter on that pebbly Provençal
beach.

———————————————————

And so it finally comes to this:

To have the luck of dying well.
Away from embarrassing soiled sheets.

Away from obscene plastic tubing
And guttural attempts for that last oxygen molecule.

A last non existential moment
When we die in front of the Other
Who will speak for us.

Hoping that the last sponge bath by a male nurse
Will make moments of levity at future family dinners…

…As the room empties itself of awareness and things.

Reflections on Le roi se meurt [Exit the King] *by Eugène Ionesco.*

A la fin de la pièce, les éléments du décor disparaîtront peu à peu jusqu'à ce que le roi disparaisse lui-même. On peut constater que tout le royaume meurt avec leur roi lors de la dernière réplique.

At the end of the play, the objects on the stage will begin to disappear little by little until the King himself disappears. We witness that the whole Kingdom dies with its King upon the last line of dialog.

TOTEMS OF THE UNIVERSE

We mistakenly live our lives within the hardened pieces
Of virtual projections of what we think we are.

Taking the unsympathetic solidity of one
As a validation of the importance
Of the very weakness of our status.

We deny the temporal softness of our beings
And take refuge in the heavy furniture of the Universe around us.

We take solace in the firmness of the products
That give support to the fragility of our organic flesh.

Lords of all our surroundings,
We read in the submission of earth, water and fire at our feet,
Their recognition of our importance as reflective beings.

Yes! We are indeed at the top of the heap.
The very symbols of the accumulation of material things.

All that, carefully fills the voids around our susceptibilities
By encasing us from the dangers of being jostled into awareness.

King of the castle, are we!
As we survey the back patio and the pretentious manicured lawn,

With leftovers of summer light conversation in our ears
And real Chablis with the ever present hint of flint.

———————————————

That is when our witty selves feel a certain envy
Toward the very non-animation of things.

The more petrified, the more banal,
The more removed from the meaningful and clever,

The more dumb and deaf, the more stone-fully still,
The more anti human, non-humanistic,

The more distant from wanting to impose anything on anything…

...the bigger the envy.

For... at the edge of that manicured lawn
That is to say... at the end of his Universe,

Walking along a stone wall, it occurred to him,
That, untold years from now, these large stones would still be around.

And, to their descendants, would be more verbal,
In their chemical density, than anything that man could write or compose.

These rocks would be present...
...as integral parts of their very own definition.

They will not need the glance of Others as intermediaries.

They would be the exemplar of immortal irony
Of absolute existential existence:

These rocks would need no one's gaze or esteem
To make them exist in time, space or society.

Not pretense and no forethought.
No attempt at a better profile in the vastness and fullness of Things.

They would just... be!

And who knows? The weakening rays of the sun
Could still, in that distant future,

Gratuitously fall on the minute pieces of quartz
Negligently and disdainfully left behind on their stony surface.

Just in case a still wandering Sisyphus
Would happen to walk by.

These rocks will be the mute and dumb witnesses
In their mute and dumb petrified way,

Of the mortal Darwinian descendant
Of what will have been the evolved slime of life.

Passage from La nausée *by Jean-Paul Sartre.*

Exister c'est être là simplement... Tout est gratuit, ce jardin, cette ville et moi-même. Quand il arrive qu'on s'en rende compte, ça vous tourne le cœur et tout se met à flotter.

To exist is to simply be there... All is gratuitous, this garden, this city and myself. When one becomes aware of this, it makes you nauseous and everything starts to float.

TOTEMS DE L'UNIVERS

Nous nous trompons, vivant nos vies
Parmi les morceaux endurcis
Des projections virtuelles de ce que nous croyons être.

Acceptant face à leur solidité antipathique
Leur validation de la primauté
De la faiblesse même de notre condition.

Nous nions l'impuissance temporelle de notre existence
Et prenons refuge parmi le bois massif du mobilier de l'univers.

Nous nous consolons de sentir le support physique des choses
Qui protège la faiblesse organique de notre chair.

Seigneurs de nos terres, nous croyons distinguer,
Dans l'infériorité de la matière à nos pieds,
L'acceptation de la prédominance de la pensée humaine.

Au sommet de la pile, sommes-nous !
Les symboles de ce qui est l'accumulation des hypermarchés.

Toutes ces choses calfatent les vides faits de nos susceptibilités
Nous isolant des dangers d'être bousculés et réveillés.

Châtelain, sommes-nous !
Alors que nous regardons de notre terrasse
L'étendue immaculée d'un gazon prétentieux.

Tout cela avec des restants de conversation vaporeuse
Aux échos de bouquet de silex d'un Chablis.

C'est alors que nous… beaux esprits…
Ressentons une certaine envie
Envers l'inanimation même des choses.

Le plus pétrifié, le plus banal,
Le plus éloigné d'une signification, de l'intelligent,

Le plus muet et sourd, le plus immobilisé dans le minéral,

Le plus antihumain, non humain,

Le plus loin de vouloir imposer
N'importe quoi sur n'importe quoi…

Plus grande l'envie.

Car… en marge de cette belle pelouse,
C'est-à-dire… en marge de son univers,

Marchant le long d'un mur de pierre,
Il lui vint à l'esprit, que dans un distant futur,
Ces gros rochers seraient toujours présents.

Et que les descendants de ces pierres
Seraient plus verbaux, dans leur densité chimique,
Que n'importe quoi que cet homme aurait écrit ou composé.

Ces pierres seraient présentes…
…comme parties entières de leur propre définition.

Elles n'auraient aucun besoin du regard intermédiaire de l'Autre.

Elles seraient l'exemplaire, par excellence,
De l'immortelle ironie de l'existence existentielle absolue :

Ces pierres n'auraient aucun besoin d'attention ou d'estime
Pour leur donner vie dans le temps, l'espace ou la société.

Aucune prétention ou arrière pensée.
Pas d'effort de mieux marquer dans l'espace des choses.

Elles ne feraient… qu'être!

Et qui sait? Les rayons affaiblis du soleil
Pourraient, dans ce futur lointain,

Tomber gratuitement sur les minuscules morceaux de quartz
Négligemment et dédaigneusement abandonnés sur leur surface pierreuse,

Juste en cas qu'un Sisyphe errant

Passerait par là, par hasard.

Ces pierres seront les témoins muets et sourds,
À leur façon pierreuse muette et sourde,

De ce descendant mortel de Darwin.
De ce qui aura évolué de la boue de la vie.

Réflexion sur le passage de La nausée *de Jean-Paul Sartre :*

Exister c'est être là simplement... Tout est gratuit, ce jardin, cette ville et moi-même. Quand il arrive qu'on s'en rende compte, ça vous tourne le cœur et tout se met à flotter.

FIRST SNOW AND BIG BANG

Late December remnants of searing Summer heat.
Stray molecules of Sirocco still whirling about.

Instinctive retreat to canopied patio.
Family apéritif of refreshing Nouilly Prat over ice.

All standard
In the standard warmth of North Africa.

All common presences
In a world of prosaic comfort.

Cold… as a distant, intriguing concept
Of seemingly right of passage currency.

———————————————————

And then… It would arrive on cue.
A Christmas postcard from the "North."

Gritty evidence of fake snow
Would slide out of envelope.

Temptation of counterfeit snow
On Holiday trees in quaint Alsatian village.

Prohibited tactile knowledge
Of earthly nourishments.

Offering to him, in that other dimension,
Evidence of white sugary goodness on cooperating nature.

Idealized lack of heat: Foreign and exotic.
Elusive. Privileged and privileging.

His world of youth would yield
To the glory of the eventual First Snow of adulthood,

That, just like that first intense glance and kiss,
Would lead to a primordial burning explosion of carnal presence.

And while that first snow,
Has long melted to the residual glimmers of the past,

The passion, born of its first sight, has not.

Like those minute remnants
Of the Genesis of cosmological heat,

Their first contact
Still spins into space and time.

Until only microscopic particles will carry into eternity
The engraved commemorating magic of that instant

In symbols easily recognizable
To all who have loved and lost.

Qu'à ce reffrain ne vous remaine:
Mais où sont les neiges d'antan!

Lest I bring you back to this refrain
Oh, where are the snows of yesteryear!

François Villon: "Ballade des dames du temps jadis."

HAPPY THOUGHTS

What if we… this world…
And the dependable twenty hour store down the street,
Were to disappear?

To be… as though we had never… been.
Thus unequivocally answering a Shakespearean anguish.

Properly and militarily blown up or eradicated by disease.
Overwhelmed by our teeming presence.

Like rats in a limited space,
Stifling and chocking on our own
Secretions, productions and excrements:
Industrial, personal, radiological.

What if…
What if a civilization came to visit
Before or after all of that?
What would be the difference?

Our concept of the beautiful would be lost.
You say important things, such as imaginatively written
And placed, black notes on music sheets,
From tortured Teutonic romanticism.

Exquisitely developed plots of heartrending
Reconstructions of analysis of the humanity's
Reciprocal dealings with each other
In accusatory classical tones bouncing against Doric columns.

Chapters after splendidly fluid chapters.
Breathless burning retorts from stage left to right
In hot Southern nights, in cars of desires.

Blushing poppy fields in the warmth of impressionistic Summers
Allowing the intrusion of translucent flowered dresses.

What if… these beings … adding to the insult,
Were so much removed from us?

So far advanced?
Their very ability to travel.
Their very technical prowess
Their own self absorption.

Would have no concept or inkling?
Not the slightest way of knowing or caring,

About what we mean, or had meant,
By our presence. Absence. Non existence?

Just the noisy and cumbersome remnants and remains
Of apparently different forms of stellar dust.

Not a happy thought.

But something to keep in mind
When we add to each others' misery
Over our concept of everlasting gods.

Would we finally recognize in our human hearts,
To the detriment and insult of our daily pride,

That we have added nothing and never would
To the eternal stillness of things?

And instead show simple, if ephemeral appreciation,
To the immigrant clerk behind the counter,

At two in the morning,
For the quart of milk for the baby.

Driving at night to the convenience store

PHILOSOPHY IN A GARAGE

With a Greek Chorus background
Of innate game show on blaring television.

Sporadic rattling of air guns on wobbly rim nuts.
Nasal mumbling of obscure names reporting to main desk.

Overactive toddler crawling on dirty rug
To inattention of mother fixated on latest movie star's problem.

Intimate information from young woman on cell phone
Concerning the proclivity towards men of former school friend.

Nothing like the present. Nothing like this setting
To promote life saving daydreaming and distraction,

From the abject putrefaction of significance and worth,
From the shapeless solidity of the stillness of time.

A human perspective on this roadmap of human dead ends:

If only we were all here… in this existential room,
In this, Sartre's space of No Exit,

If only we were here to repair our decrepitude.
To exchange our weakened original parts…

…For newer and more useful ones,

And make this sad mechanical place
The equivalent of a purposeful, vibrant Purgatory.

ALEXIS DE TOCQUEVILLE, REVISITED

"Better a smart critic than a dumb friend."
Thoughts on my adopted country.

Preemptively hearing previous remarks across the cafeteria table:
"You French... don't like us!"

Hear this, then... because... I... like you.

As a skeptic about absolutes: of things good or evil,
Admit, along with me, that your Constitution was written by men

Not elusive gods
From the province of fictitious infallibility.

Not by omniscient and immortal entities,
But by intelligent and flawed conscripts of geographical history.

That the DNA of immigrants did not mutate for the better
In the transatlantic travel: thus producing a special race of men.

Item: that the historically privileged affordability
Of copper, petroleum, cobalt, sugar... among others,

Were the compliments of a rapacious foreign policy
Enabled by a zealot CIA and corporations with flexible morals.

In the unfortunately deadly game of international puppetry
With its blood-soaked strings often manipulating brutal governments.

The children in the streets of Chile, Iran, the Congo and Cuba
Would have been the better for your neglect.

But not the neglected veteran working past retirement in dog kennels.
Not the collapsing overpasses... they... have been waiting,

Waiting for the repairs of the obscene delusional results
of Manifest Destiny
To translate into true human brotherhood.

My American friends,

Leave absolutes on the tabernacle of your worship houses.

————————————————————

In the common Judeo-Christian vocabulary
Of short script religious symbols,

Mix the essence of doubt and humility
Into the dough of your daily experience.

Let it rise and enrich your conscience and your deeds
Yes, doubt and humility.

The latter was good enough for *Job* in his lonely desert nakedness
The former for Jesus under the ominous darkness of an olive grove.

Reflections on the 'Freedom Fries' days.

IMA

Primordial cry of wounded hunter in the Savannahs of our opening years.
Reptilian fear of instinctive retreat in front of what is the Other.

Last drops of coagulating blood, divine or not, from crucified trouble makers.
Last groans of prisoner on creaky wooden rack of religious intolerance.

Gurgling sounds of weakening suspect in the police station sink.
Contradictory sounds of self righteous joy
and escaping precious temporal life
From religious sides of historic battles toward eternal void.

Animals, would be animals.

But Darwin himself would be ashamed of this addition
to his equation of evolution
At the sight of this baby's cry,

As we take the advice from Voltaire's *Candide*,
In avoiding society's intelligent, humanistic constructions
of endless repulsive ills,
By finding solace in the quiet vegetable harmony in the dirt of our gardens.

Reflection on a toddler's cry for his mother [Mumbai, November, 2008]

'Ima' is the Hebrew word for mother

GIRL FROM A SMALL NEW ENGLAND TOWN

In her college days was this seat.
Just enough natural light, just enough peace,
For rereading notes prior to tests.
Just enough background noise to stay awake.

She would rotate between these three or four seats.
Three or four tables, year after year.
These objects becoming her extended family.

Small town memories. With acrid smell of small minds.
Small town with prerequisite stereotype
Of innocence of body and spirit.

Shades of parental black and white politics and life,
Now all shades of complicated textbook grays.

And this infamous carnal knowledge of things new.
Of things that were always there,
And not new,

Since that enigmatic burning sensation
In a deep summer night,
Of a stay over during Brownies Camp.

————————————————

Now in any small coffee house
Across any academic institution,

Light years from what she was:
Awkward soccer player and Resident High School Geek.

Finally on her way to European things.
To places that wallow in lesser Clean and Clear.

Sensuality and learning had opened her
To their equivalent on other side of the universe.

Through a wormhole to where ambivalence and duality
Are concurrently possible.

A place where tiny unforeseen fault lines
Between her conscience and flesh
Had started to open up.

———————————————

Now aches in her heart from the pain
At the sight of her parents' glances.

Between Freshman year and her release into the world
Exists this gentle hammering of the mind,

That fashions beings made of small, gentle and sleepy town DNA
Into cosmopolitan replicas of questioning souls.

Absolutes about absolutes are delightfully gummed away
In boozy late night bull sessions:

"I didn't know other girls felt the same way."

New found awareness of hidden needs and covered cravings.
Until it all leads to that walk in a warm New England day.

———————————————

Pomp and Ceremony of the heart and mind.
Her folks now tearfully seem awkwardly left behind,

In the dust of family traditions.
With the chocking fumes of loving people you still love.

All in a confusion of glances
If not of strangers… then, of strangeness.

Unease about what she feels,
About what she knows, she has done,
And has been done to her.

Followed by a quasi-sad look
Of quasi-inquisition and confusion,

Of knowing maternal searching
Into her child's new soul:

"What has happened to my baby?"

The child now intellectually adult
Has cut the symbolic umbilical cord,
Belatedly, but forever.

Like virginity, it is not something that can be regained.
Gone are the days of parental absolution.

She cannot bare her soul for fear of destroying
What remains of the illusion of the past.

This coffee house, akin to a space machine,
Is a surreal object of science fiction, in space and time,

Entered for the first time,
A night of her first year,

With left over of prepubescent baby fat,
Of untouched flesh.

To emerge as a fully grown butterfly
With a beautifully spread of wings
And only pieces of yellowish cocoon left on the floor.

It's a new school year,
A new batch of students comes in for the first time.

Four years from now, like a dead skin,
They will have left, what they were, behind.

Idle thoughts while sitting in a popular university coffee shop.

QUILT: ALL THIS WISDOM ON A BED?

Angular pieces from the previously whole
Made to fit with their unknown neighbors of dissimilar genesis.

Well entrenched original identities of design and substance
Such as exotic silks and Egyptian cottons.

Embroidered filigrees and rare needle points
Of rare metals and learned representations
Forever sown intimately to each other.

Next to cloth of humble lineage and base birth
With no claim to fineries.
Maybe some discarded hardworking dungarees.

And somehow the individuality of the individual squares
Say, in a moral lesson for us all,

That the organically human, of no fiber origins,
Yes, even mankind,
Can learn from those cooperative, happy shreds,

That diversity is not incompatible with contentment.
And is much better than meaningless disintegration.

Political Sciences lessons to be learned from a quilt.

VIEW FROM THE TIP OF FOREIGN POLICIES

The gun barrel
Looked as though it were an extension of the prisoner's nose.

Two intense eyes
And a dark length of metal attached to them.

There was a ringing in the captor's ears.
His captain's almost pleading, nervous, screeching voice,
Behind, to his right side.

The soldier couldn't make out
What was being said to him.

His comrades were shouting
Properly incendiary invectives.

Acrid smells of burnt oil and flesh.
The very ground was shaking with mortar fire.

But for him,
It was complete tunnel vision and hearing
Cutting him off from his world.

If Hell was indeed around him, he was oblivious to it.
This is what must be the protective sheen for the soldier.

This cocoon of space and sound
That overwhelms senses and humanity.

So as to make the body react to only what counts:
The automatic insanity and logic of killing.

The normalization of taking
The most and only important thing from your fellow man.

And to be able to do it… mechanically… personally.

Then, to take it home.
To ponder over it with a stiff drink back at the roadside bar.
To replay it, again and again

On the shiny screen of the windshield of his car,
At night, on his way back to his inquisitive family.

He will replay everything: the smoke, the recoil.
And everything would have been fine.

Except… except the last words from the bleeding broken teeth:
Van!… Van!…

Van is a girl's name; meaning Cloud in Vietnamese.

The reader is free to substitute his or her own culturally appropriate name and setting for the consequences of Foreign Policy.

March 16, 2008, on the fortieth anniversary of the My Laï massacre, March 16, 1968.

To: Do Thi Tuyet, eight year old survivor.

EMOTIONAL PRICE

Nothing is free.
Things have a price etched on the tablets of memory

Where are kept the scores
Of Democracy's existential moments.

Its moments of commitment:
The ones that engage its future.

Making, in essence, its citizenry
Incapable of not being guilty by association.

Hiding our actions in the drapery of the voting booth
Does not hide our actions.

Lessen the shame
Nor absolve the guilt

Left, now,
Mindlessly looking at the road,

Listening to echoes of this interview.
Lifting aging dry scabs on the soul.

Wondering and in awe of the power
Of the insulating patriotic balm

That had coated this father's heart
To make him doubly blind

To the injustices of organized violence
And to a daughter's love.

We will never know the price of things
That never were or never will be.

We will never know the price of Nothing:
Such as the years of estranged silence

Between a father and daughter.

It has been said that sometimes
The least of war's cost is someone's life.

For the returning veteran continues to pay.
And nobody can pay his bill,

For the anguish
Of looking at normal life again.

For it is for the survivors to survive
And make sense of things.

To look at happy children
Knowing what had happened to their war weary brethren.

To look at pregnant women climbing on the nine o'clock bus
Knowing what was done to their African sisters.

To see pimply first baseman on a friendly baseball field
And think of his drafted uncle in Vietnamese mud.

Some survived. Some didn't.
Some cried momentarily before the end.

Some did not see anything coming,
But the survivors had to deal
With their conscience of the conscience of Things.

And nothing, nothing is more pathetic
Than the immunized immorality of a State

Coming between the love
Of a father for his child.

For this breaks the continuum
Of the universal nurturing of our young…

…Started when she found solace

In his arms during a thunder storm.

"I will never forgive that man for coming between me and my daughter."

Robin Young's father, a military man, to his estranged daughter during Watergate's Senate Hearings about President Nixon's policies, in particular the secret bombing of Cambodia.

Comment made by Robin Young about her father on her show 'Here and Now' during an interview with Joan Baez on NPR July 27, 2009

A DEVINE INDICTMENT

From the last frozen vapor crystals
Of the Gulag hard laborer.

The imploring upward glance
Of the run-away slave under the hanging tree.

From the weeping mother
Cradling a lifeless tiny bundle.

From the shattered muddy body
Of the soldier regretting long ago lips.

From all these souls
Going to meet that other side…

…One last thought, one last indictment,

If created in his own image,
The Creator should go back to work…

…Creating a new creation.

Unsolicited advice to God from a disillusioned, moribund soul.

TEST OF A CONTEMPORARY *JOB* ON WALL STREET

There came into his heart
Made of inert geometric curves,

Full of cold financial academic graphs…
…A feeling of ridicule.

Why this thought about a Biblical *Job*
Upon seeing his own milky reflection on the plastic of the screen?

Why this dusty, abstract and exterior being,
Filling up once more his empty bureaucratic hours
With literary, symbolic and distant ingredients?

But misery calling out for more misery,
It happened that, this bearded man
From the wise pages of youthful catechism, came to his mind.

Hence, in spite of luxuriating in material things.
Ties of exotic worms and silks.

Chauffeurs and concierges
With well remunerated smiles.

Friendly souls fulfilling the week ends of his superficial life.

In spite of the easy friendship of Others
Upon his being of importance,

He felt a shiver of emptiness.
Like Gilbert Bécaud's feelings…
…left with nothing at all.

His god,
The very one who had granted his Faustian demands,
Had finally rejected him.

Naked in front of his very earthly needs,
He felt overwhelmed.

Ill treated and misled.

Victim of all sorts of divine injustices and whims.

A modern *Job*,
With all the accoutrements of a good looking Bourgeois,

Facing this digital image
Made up of chemical photons.

But our original *Job*
On the sharp edged rocks of the fields of Abraham,

In spite of his biblical nudity,
Carried in, within him, in his vision,

The absolute certitude
Of an absolute divine embrace.

Eternal peace was assured
Within an indestructible paternalism.

All of this in the midst of a void and suffering
Made of temporal molecules.

While the other,
A well shaven and good looking young man,

Was left, in his mind,
With only memories of the carnal warmth of engorged lips,

Toward which he knew,
With equivalent certitude,

Having lost forever the right of touching.
In a nonetheless, immortal, non religious truth.

Crisis of Conscience faced by the Biblical Prophet Job and a Wall Street Day Trader.

Gilbert Bécaud's song 'Et maintenant...' translated in English as 'What now my love.'

MEMORIAL DAY FANTASY

Silence, respectful silence.
Truly respectful nothingness.

No canons. No shouted orders.
No fly over and ashes under.

No more idealized camaraderie
Of a pimpled buddy's last words.

Rather, the gentle fecund femininity
Of swallows flying into the breeze around the flags.

Unflinchingly honest tears and sorrow
For the ultimate message of the day:

And that is... that the dead soldiers
Of any side and all sides

Are truly dead
And will not see or know our love.

And that the day... should be turned over

To a testament of our failure
In the precious husbandry of this planet.

Another Memorial Day of Speech
May 26, 2008

Addendum: From an article in The Chronicle Review, *Section B, March 20,2009 By David P. Barash.*

On "What sports fans have in common with Nazis, male stickleback fish, and American oystercatcher.

"Our predisposition for large groups has also given birth to one of the most grotesque happenstances of human history: nationalism. When ardent nationalists convince themselves that a highly arbitrary conglomeration of tens of millions of human beings is somehow biologically or socially 'real' and deeply consequential enough to give up their lives and shed the blood of those associated with other nations – you can bet that something deep in the human psyche is being touched. Sports fans may simply be the comic sidekicks of nationalists."

AT LEAST WE WERE THIN

Black and white memory
Of black days of war.

Street scene of sane behavior of early peace.
Heavy unstylish shoes of fake leather.

Awkward cuts in coarse coats.
And ungainly dresses.

Proud dignity of women still showing
Humble sprouts of nascent femininity
Hidden and repressed by years of neglect.

Men in unorganized left over of military uniforms
With vestigial shreds where medals had been.

Precious cigarettes in fingers and mouth.
Lollypops and goodies in children's hands and hair.

Confident stare into camera from adults
With hint of cockiness given by upper sidewalk angle.

Welcome carelessness of youth
From the youngsters acting young.
They have all survived those years.

Sweet sour moments of nostalgia
From family members at holy day table.

With dry knots in their throats
And damp eyes in their way.

Observing the snapshot in grand mother's
Translucent strong knobby fingers.

Then her typical humor that had given hope
During hours of aerial night bombings

"At least, we all looked trim after years of eating rutabagas!"

Family looking at photos taken after the war.

ONCLE JULES

It was better than most other times
They usually came around two in the morning.

This time it was in the afternoon.
Lunch had been served and dishes were being put away.

Still, bombing raids are never convenient.

The drill was ingrained in everybody's brain:
To the left. Bottom of street turn right.
Run like hell to end of block and into tramway tunnel.

Sitting in the moist darkness,
Whispers and covered coughs as background.

"Where is Jules? She said.
"He went back for the wine jug"

Jules... never came back.

"He was such an incorrigible youngster... full of life" the old neighbor said.

CHITANE

His mother had warned him:
"They say that she made a pact with the Devil."

Voices from yesterday's dark cultural shadows:
Protective. Without redeeming nuances. Without further appeal.
Preparing him for future realities. Complicated and human.

Sheltering her offspring from temptations
Living in scary corners and ravines
Full of goodies enveloped in shining striated wrappers.

In this old village built upon superstitious stones.
Black dresses and eternal mourning sleeve bands,
Made of sad reasons lost in the sadness of the years.

Rumors used to float from the second floor windows.
Between the hide and seek of the hanging white wash on the lines.

The same repeated next to the tomato baskets in the old market:
Infernal slanders under the cool Summer breezes.

Her dog's name is Lucifer.
Can you believe this?

———————————————

Until the day, when a scheduling demand,
Conspiring with fatalism, always on the look out
For the fault lines in the fabric of our souls,

Replaced maternal wisdom for the moment:
And thus, he found himself seated facing this feminine rumor.

Lunch. Nothing dangerous.
Some boudin and a green salad.

But, like a scar on the soul:
The black, the green and the taste of this meal
Continued to coexist in the adult.

A necessary noon meal.

Eternal seconds. Drowning in this woman's glance.

In spite of the morning's anxious permission
Before leaving for classes.

Then, at the kitchen door,
Hearing once more, before entering,
The last echoes of familial warnings.

The wide open eyes of the adolescent could not
Push back the inexplicable alchemy of the fairytale attraction.

The animal gentleness and the natural beauty of this woman
Had laid bear the presence of bizarre and complex things.

The rich illusionary images giving birth to green sprouts
In the rich matter of the availability in this world.
Already creating sinuous waves on top of a still smooth heart.

Years later, in the middle of the permanent creases of age,
The moral dichotomy of the symbol that was this woman

Came back several times to his mind,
As he faced many other multicolored candies.

Superstitious voices in the past.

CHITANE

Sa mère l'avait prévenu :
« On dit qu'elle a fait un pacte avec le Diable. »

Voix des ténèbres culturelles d'autrefois:
Protectrices. Sans nuances rédemptrices. Sans appels.
Le préparant aux futures réalités. Compliquées et humaines.

Protégeant sa progéniture des tentations
Habitant les recoins et ravins sombres
Remplis de gourmandises aux beaux emballages striés brillants.

Dans cet ancien village aux pierres superstitieuses.
Robes noires et brassards de deuils éternels,
Aux raisons tristes oubliées dans la tristesse des années.

Les rumeurs se disaient des fenêtres du deuxième étage.
Dans le jeu de cache-cache entre le linge blanc épinglé aux cordes.

Cela se répétait près des paniers de tomates de l'ancien marché:
Des racontars infernaux sous la brise rafraîchissante d'été.

Son chien s'appelle Lucifer.
Vous vous rendez compte ?

———————————————

Jusqu'au jour, où une obligation d'emploi du temps,
Conspirant avec la fatalité, constamment aux aguets
D'éventuelles lignes de faille fragilisantes sur notre âme,

Remplaça pour le moment la sagesse maternelle:
Et, il se trouva donc assis en face de cette rumeur de féminité.

Un déjeuner. Rien de dangereux.
Du boudin et une salade verte.

Mais comme une cicatrice sur l'âme:
Le noir, le vert et le goût de ce repas
Continuèrent à coexister chez l'adulte.

Un midi à deux heures… nécessaire.

Des secondes éternelles. Noyé dans le regard cette femme.

Malgré l'approbation anxieuse du matin
Avant le départ pour les cours.

Puis, à la porte de la cuisine,
Entendant, une fois de plus, avant d'entrer,
Les derniers échos familiaux de mise en garde

Les yeux effrayés de l'adolescent n'arrivèrent pas
À repousser l'inexplicable alchimie de l'attraction féerique.

La douceur animale et la beauté naturelle de cette femme
Avaient mis à nu la présence de choses bizarres et complexes.

La richesse d'images illusionnistes engendrant des pousses vertes
Dans la matière grasse de la disponibilité dans les choses.
Faisant déjà flotter des vagues sinuant dans ce cœur encore lisse.

Des années plus tard, au milieu des plis permanents de l'âge,
La dichotomie morale du symbole de cette femme

Lui revint plusieurs fois à l'esprit,
Face aux choix de bien d'autres multicolores sucreries.

Voix superstitieuses dans le passé.

Chitane : Satan en arabe marocain.

REFLECTIONS ON *OLYMPIA* BY MANET

Multiple nuances of whites
Multiplying themselves in wavy nuptials of flesh and icy satin on the bed.
Silver clair-obscur spots of pure lithium.

Radiant carnal value of the fragility of nudity,
Offering an unexpected frankness of body and glance.

Intermediary setting, between the uniformity of African tonality
And luminous European frivolity.

Painterly echoes of understated sanguine facial blush.
Incongruous sensuality of the curves
Amidst the marble solidity of a muscular, virile femininity.

Fabulously transposed dreams of imminent savory moments
Found in the illicit depths of details of Orientalism,

Contradicted by the false modesty of the hand gesture.
All betrayed by the confidence of the face.

Happy and privileged voyeurism
Of the marriage of the primordial amoral
To the subtle temptations of puritan taboos.

Ease of sexual abandonment
In the middle of a sensuality out of our reach,
On this, the middle class side of the closed gates of Paradise.

RÉFLEXIONS SUR *L'OLYMPIA* DE MANET

Nuances multiples de blancheurs
Se multipliant sur le lit en vagues nuptiales de chair et de coton.
Couleur argentée en clair-obscur au lithium pur.

Valeur charnelle radieuse de la fragilité du nu,
Offrant une franchise surprenante du corps et du regard.

Scène intermédiaire entre l'uniformité tonale africaine
Et la frivolité lumineuse européenne.

Échos de touches sanguines sous entendues sur les pommettes.
Sensualité incongrue des courbes
Dans la solidité de marbre d'une féminité musclée et virile.

Rêves fantaisistes transposés à des moments à venir savoureux
Trouvés dans les profondeurs illicites des détails orientalistes.

Contredits par la fausse pudeur du geste de la main
Trahi par la franchise du visage.

Voyeurisme heureux et privilégié
Du mariage du primordial amoral
Aux tentation subtiles des tabous puritains.

Abandonnement facile sexuel
Au milieu d'une sensualité hors de notre portée
De ce côté bourgeois du portail fermé du Paradis.

THE TEACHER... A CULTIVATED NOMAD

The teacher is a cultivated nomad
Surrounded by the waves of a vaguely determined destiny.

In front of her,
Lost, meandering, sharp edged paths.
Natural and man made obstacles and impasses.

Surviving often on only the fluids of personal Will.
Drawing sustenance from her leather pouch of ideals.

The very same personal visions which protect
From the perilous solar rays of society's disdain or fear of Humanism.

Keeping the directional faith of the value of true professionalism.
Through the reward of the intellectual intimacy of communication.

Imparting knowledge to the Other... the Student.

Courage. In spite of moments of fatigue as the years go by.
All made up, in the desert setting sun of a career,
By the salvation of the unctuous juices of one day's fruitful lesson.

All the basic nourishment for survival
Found in the rich wheat of that Culture.
Its earthly Wisdom. The Manna of the learning process.

The professor. The symbol.

In honor of the profession

THE LASCAUX CAVES

Somewhere in the recombined air mixture of the future,
In some distant time, in some sterilized room,

A man will pick up a digitized brush
And draw fantasies of the past.

On his electron fed screen
Will evolve, from his internet fed memory,

Idealized and quasi magical scenes
Of shaded vibrant forests and green molecular growths.

Fantastic artificial academic recollections of chronicled accounts
Of things past. Dangerous to absorb and understand.

Images… destructive for their depressing appeal,
And useless for their practical impossibility.

Such things as walks with naked feet on pliable blades of grass,
Deep blue Mediterranean sheets lapping at reddish rocks.

Wide eyed game in search of shade,
And elegant swans as wavy lithium watery forms.

This man, made partially of computer chips
And artificially extended life, safe in his deep underground habitat,

Away from mortal solar and gamma winds,
Depleted oxygen and deserted environment,

Will, in turn, paint, in his modernistic electronic "cave"
Memories of another world.

Will he have a brief and envious thought
About his fur covered freezing ancestor in his Lascaux cave?

For those muddy images of animals were at least
Within easy reach outside of that prehistoric cave.

Reflection on Soylent Green's scene before suicide when the dying candidate sees images of a luxuriant nature, now vanished.

TO LIVE IN THE MOMENT

The everyday marvel of the marvel of everyday.
To see, to sense, the surprise of the first time,
Every time.

Seeing the same house, entering the same door way,
To stroke the silky coat of the family golden retriever,
For the first time, every time.

To marvel at the reflection of the sun across the filigree of leaves.
The sheen on the front yard lawn of one's house,
For the first time, every time.

To discover the existence of a teary eyed brother
In the person standing at the bottom of the parental stairs,
For the first time, every time.

But missing what poets want:
The lyrical reconstruction, the artistic quest, the need to rebuild,

The breathless pursuit, even to human exhaustion,
Of what it is to be human:

To be, once more, under that loving glance.

Not through a mindless rewinding mechanism.
But rather seeing something for the first time,

While still feeling the burning embers,
Of the awareness, of that other first time.

Reflection on Gustav Molaison whose medical short term memory retention condition made him feel everything for the "first time."

DON'T LOOK BACK

The very picture of living in the moment:
Provençal sunlight still worthy of Van Gogh.

Obedient sunflowers following their namesake in the Azure.
Distant hints of lavender beds and green stains of vineyards
In the soporific hills full of the sound of the cicadas.

Not a hint of impending doom.
Not a care about the next seconds or years.

Just the perfumed remnants of the essences of a world
Pregnant with the immediacy of stimulated senses.

The goodness of being alive.
The luxuriousness of earthly nourishments…

Three feet away from the one hundred and thirty speed limit.

Observation of a dog running on the Autoroute in Southern France

ALTERNATE UNIVERSE

In the true definition of the definition of oneself,
It is in the negation of existence
That things and actions take their meaning.

Not having a moment after a certain moment:
A certain incident. A certain accident.

A missed sharp turn in the darkness of a university party.
An aborted descent on top of a plane.

The avoided death in an aggression
In the void and desperation of an urban street
Prevented by the thickness of a collar.

And things would have ended.
At thirty, twelve, sixteen. Whatever.

No more to add to the definition of a definition.
To the violence or gratuity of happenstance.

No further hint of the rich organic human presence
In the other forks in the road. Those other ways.
That other universe of things and possibilities.

———————————————

Scheduling error and missing the infamous plane.
White reflector at the very last moment.

Turning your head sideways to glance at a window:
Just hearing the flight of the bullet.

Faith and death. Happiness or blank slates.
Something and nothing
Not even deigning a look toward each other.

Not a glance or a care
From these determining pieces of Time and Space.

Complete unanimated stupidity
Of the different colors of the casino wheel

Of people and events. Good… and bad.

Doing and stopping. Casino wheel that we try to gum up
By burning the wax of church candles.

Or burning others for their contradictory beliefs
In the hope of opening up our own protective umbrella.

Then… there is the memory, while in that plane,
Of an old woman with milky biblical eyes:

"You know what?"
"I have seen and experienced enough during the war."

"Faith cannot do more to me."
"Don't worry. We'll be fine."

Said with the same hard conviction
As the solidity of the sweaty plastic armrest.

Nothing happened.
Faith must have had given up… that day.

When one's Faith is one's Fate

IN THE THIRD PERSON

Syntax in a letter that reflects back to its surprised reader.
Visions in a seemingly distorted mirror of malefic images.

Microscopic faults in his soul revealed
Through the lens of her anguish.

Verbally scrapping away his self serving varnish
From his every flaws.

Abandoned. Left alone. Beyond naked… nude
In front of this verbal, unblinking, omniscient mirror

Asking his chaste hand to cover unwelcome feelings:
"Who is this person?"

Emotional third person
Removing him as the object of the verb
In spite of his being the subject at hand.

The whole exercise turning into
A sort of voyeuristic view of himself

Leaving him wondering about
The nature of his nature
And the new definition of the truth.

Fearful glance toward this spectral Doubleganger
Full of reciprocal self damnation.

———————————————————

This time… no mere theoretical academic concept
Of a clever literary viewpoint.

Voyeuristic divorce. Syntax made of mirrors.
The object of scorn is indeed, the subject.

Attempts by this fine mind
And failed human being

To find proper solutions

For this angst as the observer of his own deeds.

Admitting now, of not being worthy
Of being in someone's daughter's arms

Having the soul of a beast.
But no Beauty to redeem him.

"Could I be that person?"

Sharp edges of the psychological description
Contrasting with the softness of his self delusion.

Existential nausea. Bile of the spirit.
For having caused such pain.

Long gone now the romanticized first person of loving words
As the object of her decimated affection.

Reflections on some of the men in Jane Austen's novels.

THE KEYBOARD

Picturing her standing
In front of the full length mirror,

Adjusting the thin black straps
Around her porcelain shoulders.

A sideway glance at her figure
And understated breasts.

A knock on the door and then a walk
Through blood red velvet curtains

Onto the venerable oak wood of European stage.
Fruitlike lights from historic candelabras.

Angelic sway and his reminiscence
Of naked muscular flesh on the way to a waiting bench.

Murmurs of anticipation
And complete professional concentration.

Electric contact
With warm ivory and hammering left hand

Sensual tantalizing
Of crystalline notes from the plaintive right hand.

Aggressive volume from play of the pedals
From inside the masculine curves of a grand piano.

Unconditional abandonment of inner metal strings
To the exquisite torture of her precious touch.

Shameless proof of her total bodily offering
To this wooden rival for her love in front of a nameless ornate hall.

Leaving him, dry mouthed and envious of the television image
Of this infernal musical machine

That knows nothing

Of the value of her caresses under cotton sheets.

Hoping a Mephistopheles figure
Would appear over the coffee fumes of his cup

To bargain in an instant
For his eternal damnation

Gladly sold for a few more moments
As inert keys under her slender fingertips.

"I'm staying late at the office to process some folders."

Epitaph of Modern Society

"...Laisse-moi devenir / L'ombre de ton ombre / L'ombre de ta main / L'ombre de ton chien..."

"...Let me become / The shadow of your shadow / The shadow of your hand / The shadow of your dog..."

Ne me quitte pas *by Jacques Brel*

PART II

DROPLETS OF TIME

MIMOSAS

Happiness and contentment disguised themselves
That afternoon, after lunch, and burst into his life.

It was made of the yellow powdery softness
From the little perfumed spheres of the moment.

Happy is he who can simply reach up
And take an armful of mimosa branches.

Get down from the side of the wall
Shake the yellow dust from his shirt

And proudly offer these symbols
Of a gentle nature that knows how to exist only in youth.

A privileged time made more so after these years
By the awareness that something special

Was sitting on the side of the teacher's desk
That one afternoon in the resplendent sun of Africa.

Morocco

Illustration by Katy Norman.

LES MIMOSAS

Ce jour-là, après le déjeuner, le bonheur et la satisfaction
Se déguisèrent et envahirent sa vie.

Ils se manifestèrent sous une douce forme poudreuse jaune
Sous l'apparence de petites sphères parfumées du moment.

Heureux celui qui peut en simplement ouvrir ses bras
Les remplir de branches de mimosas.

Descendant de l'autre côté du mur
On secoue la poussière jaune.

Heureux celui qui offre fièrement ces symboles
D'un monde de douceur qui seul sait exister dans la jeunesse.

Un moment rendu plus privilégié par les années.
Et la conscience qu'une présence spéciale

Se trouvait sur la table de l'institutrice
Cet après midi-là, dans le soleil resplendissant d'Afrique.

Maroc

OF BIBLICAL ANCESTRY AND NUDE BEACHES

Wild open spaces of untamed passions:
Unrestrained white horses and black bulls of salt marshes.

Enduring tolerance for complexity of behavior and beliefs.
Agnosticism toward the laws of man from wandering Gypsies.

Touching religious festivals of dubious folklore.
Speculation of blue blooded divine ancestry.

All sides of human richness coexisting amid
The essences of saffron dishes,

Sweating wine carafes and pungent tomato sauces,
Cloudy Pastis and brittle baguettes.

Traditional long Arlésienne colorful dresses
Along translucent white cotton temptations.

Privileged solar setting for hymn to rich expressions.
Of spirit and flesh. Pounding veins and passionate beliefs.

All in a precious and earthly balance
Between the wrought iron church Campaniles
And the relaxed hedonism of bare flesh on white sand.

Reflection on the little town in Camargue of Les Saintes Maries de la Mer where, according to tradition, the fleeing Mary Magdalene, Mary Salome and Mary Jacob came ashore.

WHAT REALLY COUNTS

And now... something really important:
No economic disasters. No political clashes.

Religious strives are nothing.
Bigotry and intolerance are secondary.

Children buried under the rubble of collateral damage,
Violated women running out of destroyed villages.

Ocean temperature and polar ice cap
Going in opposite directions.

What will it all eventually mean?

What counts is how things happened.
Things! Why should they be?

Why should there be something instead of nothing?
And what is nothing? Is it something?

I'm going to think really hard.
Think... nothing. Think... void.

My head hurts.

Today, la Baie des Anges is a typical deep Mediterranean blue:

"Mademoiselle... un autre kir s'il vous plaît."

Among and of heavenly bodies on the flat stones of La promenade des Anglais *in Nice.*

AT EASE WITH ONESELF

At times, like multicolored butterfly wings
With overflowing summer dresses.

Or shiny black miniskirted fearless damsels.
Displaying gently, muscular legs when stopped at red lights.

These, the descendants of heavy armored medieval Knights.
These women, in turn, now exuding urban bravery,

Along with self-possessed, self-driven satisfaction
For the World to see... or not...
...Such seems to express their Parisian pout.

With positive energy everywhere:
For the greening of the earth,
And healthy benefit of flowing air.

Observation of Parisian femininity on bicycles.

BEGINNINGS... AND THE END

Multitude of ancestral possibilities
For the rest of us, mere mortals.

Unlike royal blood with some textbook tracing
We... we read chronicles of centuries and wonder:

What part of us was part of these parts?

Did he fight the Ottoman Empire?
Was he helping the King of Naples get on his horse?

Was she the illegitimate daughter of a Prussian officer:
A Venetian beauty with incongruous Nordic green eyes?

Between the anthropological Eve of Africa
And this Grecian Gallic city,

Was it a preparation for one of them
To sail off, one night, from Camargue,

To stand in front of the walls of Jerusalem,
And make a statement for religious domination?

Or had one of his ancestors, instead, stood idly by
As a Jewish renegade Rabbi fell for the third time?

How many dead ends of family trees
Did it almost take to arrive to one of us?

How many times did the reptile brain,
Of any of these people of the above hanging branches,

Come to the rescue of that precious DNA?
To kill and to survive for another day?

To conveniently produce another offspring
One the eve of a fatal battle?

This roulette wheel of life and death
That mindlessly would create this one being... us.

In an effort of the willing and unwilling.
In the ambivalence of purposeful action and gratuitous inaction.

Minuscule protoplasm in the pastoral mud of Italian hills,
Or a surprised Norman fisherman glancing at Richard the Lionheart...

And then comes the moment that none of us can share.
It is done in the soundproof intimacy of complete loneliness...

...we die.

All this serendipity of ancestral solidarity
Interpreted as directional and important.

We somehow want our pound of fame
To impose our existence on succeeding ones.

A piece of cemetery real estate and a granite seal
For our pompous heart and weak body.

Hoping it will make a difference
Two thousand years from now.

Heard at the cafeteria table

"In a hundred years, no one will give a crap."

RECIPROCAL VISIONS

Another nonchalant glance to the left, in a routine moment:
An old man struggling with a recalcitrant store carriage.

Same deformed back previously seen in the vegetable section.
Same attempt at ignoring the threatening icons of my future.

Damn! Why I am slowing down?
Even the automatic door wants me out.

Twisted finger tips and flopping plastic bags.
Unstable posture looking for a piece of solidity.

I hear: "May I help you?"
From an unstoppable, surprising side of me. Of us.

And a barely audible, gentle and fragile as snow answers:
"No! Thank you!"

But his glance... was splendid.
The same that prophets must have taken to their deaths.

Just as delusional. Just as romanticized.
But human to its core and meaning.

I wondered if he had had the same experience
As a young man and was seeing the moment repeating itself.

Transferring into my soul
A message and a responsibility for my own future.

MANIFESTO FOR GENTLE SOULS

Gentle souls of the world, unite and multiply.
Find each other's glance in a crowd.

Discover the match of your mutual fear
In this sea of extroverted humanity.

In that corner of a cocktail party
Between the book shelf and the lamp,

Instinctively decipher the whispers
On the other's lips among the booming guitar bass line.

Elegantly ignore the snickering remarks of office friends
Referring to your lack of social graces.

While the other beautiful people
Keep finding multiple voids in meaningless dialogs,

You softly lay out your remembrance
Of your respective love

Of the solitary walks you took in your lonely youth…
…At least, until this pivotal moment.

Two quiet souls at a cocktail party.

THE GRANITE WALL

The other side of the granite wall,
The one made of everything that she isn't.

Flesh eating and soul breaking roughness
Made of petrified human disregard.

The wall of coagulated streaks of blood
From his unsuccessful climbing attempts.

Hearing now idyllic noises streaming above his head
From unreachable walled off happiness.

Rustling sounds of intimate joy
Of what he can conceive is a luxurious bed of soft blades of grass.

While on his side of the wall an eternal solar eclipse
Makes gray shadows out of shy silhouettes.

His mind reconstructs bloated red lips
Emanating from the silt of pleasure from this so close fruitful land.

Visions of the tears of Don José for his Carmen
Sobs for a better ending in the Bridges of Madison County.

A last second entrance of a Juliet for her Romeo.
A glance of acknowledgment in Doctor Zhivago.

All these scenes bring on the sentence, even for a fleeting moment,
Of the awareness of a secular purgatory on Earth:

That is, emotional isolation and the knowledge, the knowledge,
Of loss and the impossibility of retrieval.

Like looking at miniscule ripples of grains of sand
And knowing the time of high tide.

Beyond the End.

REMEMBRANCE OF SPRING GRASS

Like a toggle switch in his mind
Having gone to blind setting.

On its own. On its very own,
While he was busy rationalizing.

The synapses of remembrance ignoring their responsibilities.
That of keeping alive the love and the face of the lover.

A secular trinity in his life that had been made of
Gentle embrace... unconditional acceptance... ever present forgiveness.

Synapses that could recreate,
At his leisure, at his demand... at his whims,

The angles, the shadows, the creases,
Pliability of forms and things

Of a past filtered by a curve hugging veil
Made of the silk of yesterday's secretions.

Remembrance of things and people.
Minute and expansive:

The semi transparence of dew on Spring grass
Acting as a magnifying glass on the veins of the blades.

Mineral and organic compositions
Of nuptial smells of cosmological dimensions

That offer to lovers the vision
Of blushing flesh and surprised glances

Of the precious waning seconds just beyond ecstasy
That hint of inner life comprised of immortal seconds.

The birth of a smile after the sadness
In the crimping at the corner of the lips.

All that gone.

A blindness of the soul.

Leaving him aimlessly walking
Into the invisible walls of culpability.

Fear and loneliness roaming the empty voids
Of the reverberating dry arterial walls of the present.

Death and its dryness have taken over
The faded green carpet of Paradise.

The ex-lover left brooding
Over his cooling cup of coffee,

While the only remnants of sight left to the sightless,
Is that of darkened rusted metallic silhouettes.

Burnt shells of passion. Burnt by their own passion.
Ugly bags of ugly cloth spread on the microbial floor.

Trash receptacles full of thoughtless moments and actions
Now dead weights of existential guilt

"Did I ever think of her?"

Like a disaster movie fiction script
Calling for going to full black on the screen.

Leaving the audience in a Bergman stupor
With just images of shredded pieces of flesh and soul.

HOW TO WASTE YOUR LIFE

The shyness of the moon came out last night
And he… ignored it.

He was too busy avoiding
The gaping holes in the darkness of his routine.

Dogs were barking aimlessly at slamming doors
As people decided to watch reality on their television sets instead.

A timid breeze was going through the leaves
But the wisdom of its sound
Was countered by the noise of his wristwatch.

The impressionistic vitreous clinking
Of a channel bell at the entrance of the marina
Was only able to remind him of his lateness for supper.

And in his digitized mind, it occurred to him
That the gentle cypress tops in the eternity of the cemetery
Had the uncanny aggressiveness of phallic symbols.

Once in the artificial safety of his room
He could smell the wetness of the new grass
Through the opened window…

…He mechanically went back to his electronic screens
To look for his electron fed dependable escape.

VOYAGE: MAKING THE BEST OF THINGS

It was morning and the sun was setting.
The clock in the kitchen was saying so.

This morning's sun saw its shadow
And decided to let the moon take over.

Children's laughter was absorbed
By the cooling petals of the afternoon park.

Everything comes to an end.

A ship docks or flounders
But it ends up somewhere.
And those on board have no say as to which.

Eternal world of eternal feelings
Peel off the walls of hope
And their fall make a hollow sound.

Word came in today that part of the world had died.
No one had told me. But I could still feel it.

I had thought my pieces of it were hiding. But I was wrong.
I had been robbed and had to accept it.

It feels as though a giant equation is in charge of things
And the value for "x" is imaginary.

But I still scribble attempts at a solution.
But in pencil. Just in case I think I hear whispers of an answer.

The kiss, the near fatal incident,
The last second correction on that dark curve,
The bullet hitting the collar instead of the temple,

Were just stops on the way home.
The doorway would have been the same color anyway.
Once in, I will look for familiar faces
But find only mirrors.

So I will have to entertain myself
By making faces.

It's not all that bad. It could have been worse.
It could have been nothing.

Reflections on the poem 'Spleen' by Charles Baudelaire.

TRYING TO UNDO THINGS

It happened at the Gate of Appeal and Joy,
At the natural opening into Things.

Slipping into a comfortable hedonism akin to a warm bath
With floating petals of untouched flowers.

Instinctive animal norm confronting
The codified complexity of society.

The pounding noise of the excited heartbeats in the temples
Obliterating the last shouts from a higher existential conscience.

Sounds of wisdom. Hoarse and beaten down.
Discarded and forgotten along the path.

All was well under the convenient breezes of self absorption.

Until the day, the second... when words... a poignant phrase,
Showed him the emotional chaos that had been left behind.

A scene of the irremediably broken state of ethereal presences:

The quivering carnal genesis of a smile.
The girlish trust behind a searching glance.
A barely audible gasp preceding unconditional abandonment.

Man of the world. Boulevardier in his own mind.
He looked around for the first time.

Divested shards of precious body crystals.
Scattered powdered gold from her glistening bosom.
Riches, all of them, from a bruised soul.

Loving confessional dialogs of yesterday.
Mined religiously for lyrical wealth, today.

These pieces of human decency and integrity,
Burnt in the caldron of the heat of the moment,
To extract distilled phantoms of the solidity of the past.

All this self-satisfaction now incinerated in an instant
By the gentle, non-accusatory purity of these simple words:

"This pain made me grow up."

Emotional innocence is spent but only once,
Being the valuable, fragile currency of the virtue of youth.

———————————————————

While his pain and guilt will continue to be of this earth
With every glance returned by… that glance,

Knowing that nothing will be waiting for him on the other side
But eternal, anguish free, unforgiving emptiness.

Reflections on Ingmar Bergman's Scenes from a Marriage.

EFFORT POUR REMÉDIER AUX CHOSES

Cela se passa à la Porte du charme et de la joie,
Au passage naturel dans les Choses.

Rentrant dans un hédonisme similaire à un bain tiède
Où flottaient des pétales de fleurs vierges.

Mœurs instinctives animales confrontant
La complexité codifiée de la société.

Le battement excité du cœur dans les tempes
Oblitérant les derniers cris du haut d'une conscience existentielle.

Des sons de sagesse. Rauques et affaiblis.
Rejetés et oubliés le long du sentier.

Tout était bien sous la brise accommodante du narcissisme.

Jusqu'au jour, la seconde, quand des mots… une phrase poignante,
Lui montra les restes d'un chaos émotionnel.

Une vision de la destruction irrémédiable de présences éthérées :

Le tremblement charnel à la genèse d'un sourire.
La confiance d'une fillette dans le regard inquisitorial.
Un soupçon de soupir précédant l'abandonnement sans conditions.

Homme débonnaire. Boulevardier selon lui-même.
Pour une fois, il observa son alentour.

Éclats de cristaux corporels précieux… rejetés.
Poudre éparpillée de l'or de ses seins scintillants.
Le tout fait des richesses d'une âme meurtrie.

Tendres dialogues confessionnels d'hier.
Exploités religieusement aujourd'hui pour leur valeur lyrique.

Ces morceaux de décence et d'intégrité humaines
Brûlés dans le four chauffé à la chaleur du moment,
Pour en distiller les fantômes de la solidité du passé.

Tout cet amour-propre maintenant incinéré en un instant
Dans la douce pureté non accusatrice de ces simples mots :

« Cette douleur m'a rendue plus sage. »

L'innocence émotionnelle ne se dépense qu'une fois,
Étant la monnaie chère et fragile de la vertu de la jeunesse.

———————————————————

Alors que pour lui, sa peine et culpabilité continueront d'être de ce monde
Avec chaque regard… de ce regard,

Sachant que rien d'autre ne l'attendra de l'autre côté
Que le néant éternel, non angoissant, mais sans pitié.

Réflexions sur Scènes d'un mariage *de Ingmar Bergman.*

EMOTIONAL VOYEURISM

Nailed to the floor of passivity, he sees himself in the Other.
In the anonymous future of the splendid moments of this Other.

Tool of his own agony, of his perversion,
The unfiltered eye talks about images in images.

What is. What will never be.
He comes nearer.

He hears echoes of burning things known to him.
A former initiated, he sees once more the familiar curves.

From a half opened door he witnesses untouchable gifts
In the shadow of his own shame.

Protecting his dignity.
Holding in his arms a mirage of tenderness.

The right to a biblical intimacy lost long ago
In the buzzing noise of the collapse of the walls of Paradise.

No more confession escaping from reddened cheeks.
No more promising smile. No more multiple realities,

Offering the richness of decisive moments
With variable existentialist futures.

Left are the fear to know and the need to see,
Behind the hidden doors of jealousy and heart.

Seeing one's silhouette in the mirror of Things
Living through the words that provoke the shiver
Of the precious down in this reflection of the nape.

Incongruously masochistic vision coming to his mind,
While observing two zigzagging butterflies
In the nuptial warmth of Summer.

Daydreaming far from the dream.

VOYEURISME ÉMOTIONNEL

Cloué au parquet de la passivité, il se voit en l'Autre.
Dans l'anonymat futur des moments splendides de cet Autre.

Outil de son agonie, de sa perversion,
L'œil sans filtre dit les images en images.

Ce qui est. Ce qui ne sera plus.
Il s'approche.

Il entend des échos de choses ardentes connues de lui.
Ancien initié, il revoit les courbes familières.

D'une porte entrouverte il est témoin d'offres intouchables
À l'ombre de sa propre honte.

Sauvegardant sa dignité.
Tenant dans ses bras un mirage de tendresse.

Le droit à l'intimité biblique perdu il y a longtemps
Dans le bourdonnement du bruit de l'écroulement des murs du paradis.

Plus d'aveu s'échappant de joues rougies.
Plus de sourire annonciateur. Plus de multiples réalités,

Offrant la richesse de moments décisifs
Aux futurs variables existentiels.

Restent la peur de savoir et le besoin de voir,
Derrière la jalousie des portes et du cœur.

Voir sa silhouette dans le miroir des choses
Vivre à travers les mots qui font maintenant trembler
Le duvet précieux de la réflexion de cette nuque.

Vision masochiste incongrue lui venant à l'esprit
En observant deux papillons zigzagant
Dans la tiédeur nuptiale d'été.

Rêverie loin du rêve.

SO CLOSE AND YET SO FAR

Imperceptible sighs from the object of desire
Hidden from the glance of the gods
Who had only been able to force feed him with crumbs of void.

Gone, the weight of this presence on his own chest
Acting as a contretemps to cherished heart beats.

Holding his breath to prevent the disappearance
Of the leftover of youth among the down of the nape of the neck.

In his arms, he had seen the consciousness of the ephemeral
Letting itself be discerned in the eyes full of so much trust
In the timid solar light of the curtains.

So close… and yet, so far.

To be envious of everything… and of nothings.
Of absurd and gratuitous things, past and future.

Jealous of human fevers already known of him
That she would know henceforth without him.

These passions with no preconception.
With no restrictions. With no tomorrows.

Nectars that let themselves be swallowed like the last sobs
Of the last moments of ecstasy.

These same whose aftertaste
Never last long enough on our lips.

So close… and yet, so far.

Everything… and then, emptiness on the chest.
Without this precious weight which had asked nothing for itself.

The irony of not having dared to eat enough
Of the earthly nourishments

Seeping through the too large temporal mesh.

Pearls of happiness now liquid
Drying on the fabric of the soul

Multilayered presence:
Quavering. Aggressive. Half virginal.

Divine and infernal alchemy. Celestial and silty.

Giving to human things
The splendid richness of the complexity that is life.

Half virginal: this reddish shade of the cheekbones.
Half virginal: this intense and curious glance.

Like this nervous gesture toward an invisible object on the table:
Immediately preceding the confession, audible only by lovers.

This place of the Happy Few that makes a single soul from two
Now naked in front of their object all of desires
Making redundant any others.

Black cosmological hole. Elementary force
Which erase time.

Half virginal. Half touched.
This fold of the eyelids. This fold of the lips.

That let us discover the shadow of a little girl
Anxious: not wanting to suffer.

So close... and now so far.

First pangs of sensuality: reflections on Françoise Sagan.

SI PROCHE... ET SI LOIN

Soupirs imperceptibles de l'objet de désir
Caché au regard des dieux
Qui, eux, n'avaient su le gaver que de miettes de néant.

Disparu, le poids de cette présence sur sa propre poitrine
Servant de contretemps au battement du cœur aimé.

Retenant son souffle de peur que ne s'envolent
Les restants de jeunesse parmi le duvet de sa nuque.

Dans ses bras, il avait vu la conscience de l'éphémère
Se laisser deviner dans ces yeux remplis de tant de confiance
Dans la timidité solaire des rideaux.

Si proche... et pourtant si loin.

Être envieux de tout... et des riens.
De choses absurdes et gratuites, passées et futures.

Jaloux des fièvres humaines déjà connues de lui.
Qu'elle connaîtra dorénavant sans lui.

Ces passions sans arrière pensé.
Sans restriction. Sans lendemain.

Nectars qui se laissaient avaler comme les derniers sanglots
Des derniers moments de l'extase.

Ceux dont l'après goût
Ne languit jamais assez longtemps sur nos lèvres.

Si proche... et pourtant si loin.

Tout... et puis la poitrine vide
Sans ce poids précieux qui ne demandait pas plus.

L'ironie de ne pas avoir oser assez se nourrir
De nourritures trop terrestres

S'égrainant à travers les mailles temporelles trop grandes.

Des perles de bonheur devenues liquides
Se sèchent sur la housse de l'âme.

Présence feuilletée :
Tremblante. Agressive. Mi vierge.

Alchimie divine et infernale. Céleste et boueuse.

Donnant aux choses humaines
La splendeur et riche complexité de la vie.

Mi vierge : cette rougeur sur les pommettes des joues.
Mi vierge : ce regard intense et curieux

Comme ce geste nerveux vers un objet invisible sur la table:
Juste avant l'aveu que seuls les amants entendent.

Le lieu des happy few qui fait une âme de deux
Maintenant nue devant l'objet de tous désirs
Rendant superflus tous les autres.

Trou noir cosmologique. Force élémentaire
Qui fait oublier le temps.

Mi vierge. Touchés à moitié,
Ce pli des paupières. Ce pli des lèvres,

Qui laissaient découvrir l'ombre d'une fillette
Inquiète de souffrir.

Si proche…et maintenant si loin.

Les premières brindilles de sensualité : réflexions sur Françoise Sagan.

DROPLETS OF TIME

It was the incongruity of the setting.
Bitter sweet carnal wisps of her, reconstructed faithfully
On his lips and in his nostrils.

The vapors of remembrance were perfect.
The middle of the kitchen was not.

Wanting to test the warmth of the soup
He had put a sample in his mouth.

The voluptuousness of the substance
Put the past back on the clock.

Her flesh on his mind.
The syrupy balm of immortality on his soul.

Tart raspiness of greens. Blend of sugary potato gentleness.
Unction from the robe of heavy cream and real butter.

Unaware faithful molecular cousins of bodily distilled essence.
These elementary ingredients.
These distant, disinterested culinary things,

Somehow converted the cold linoleum space,
In front of the stainless steel stove,

Into the place where he had first filled his lungs
With the similar ephemeral incense of happiness
Made of purified virile femininity.

And Man created Vichyssoise.

GOUTTELETTES DU TEMPS PASSÉ

C'était plutôt l'incongru du site.
Des brins charnels aigres-doux, la restituant fidèlement
Sur ses lèvres et dans ses narines.

Les vapeurs du souvenir étaient parfaites,
Le milieu de la cuisine ne l'était pas.

Voulant déterminer la chaleur de la soupe
Il en avait mis dans sa bouche.

La volupté de la substance
Remit le passé à l'horloge,

Sa chair dans son esprit,
Le baume sirupeux de l'immortel dans son âme.

Acerbité râpeuse des légumes.
Mélange de richesse sucrée des pommes de terre.
Velouté enrobé de crème et de beurre.

———————————————————

Cousins moléculaires inconscients d'essence corporelle distillée.
Ces ingrédients élémentaires.
Ces choses culinaires distantes, désintéressées,

Parvinrent à transformer l'espace de linoléum froid,
Face à la cuisinière en inox,

En l'endroit où il avait pour la première fois rempli ses poumons
De l'encens éphémère similaire au bonheur
Fait de féminité virile purifiée.

Et l'Homme créa la Vichyssoise.

THE TASTE OF SNOW

Sitting on a snow covered picnic bench,
Steam rising from my opened coat,
Muscles aching from unaccustomed shoveling,

Freezing whiteness,
Incongruous desert like thirst,

I put a glove full of snow to my mouth,
Tasting of the emptiness of elemental purity.

Realizing that the chaotic chemical taste
From the good dirt of this earth

Will make the lowly French crew member,
The one in the cooking galley,
The most important space traveler.

The one with vials of precious herbal essences
From the hills of Provence.

The one with natural flavors of sauce bourguignonne.
The one with emanations of black truffles
In sealed plastic bags,

To add to smart, but molecular reconstructions
Of meats and vegetables.

Thus giving the future of our race...

...a past.

French Cuisine and Space Travel

ANOTHER LIFE, ANOTHER TIME

Reflections of moist thoughts
On the vapors of early morning Spring dew.

Fleeting images among the streaks
On a windshield in the night.

Distracting left over of that voice,
While reading a solitary newspaper,

On solitary bench with the shivering feeling
Of invisible flesh against lonely flesh.

Time is… a quarter past you.
It was here and is gone.

Physics and minutes being what they are,
No amount of wishing will warp their laws in your favor.

Dead electrons and dying molecular cells
Contain only disinterested solidity.

While under the sheen of the surface rationalism of fatalism,
Our heart can still discern a crowded world of other things:

The teaming of life in the rich pond of dreams.

Deep where human hope… and only deluded human hope,
Dares to inhale the narcotic illusion of delusion.

That alternate second chance
Of another life. Another time.
That hangs temptingly close to cracked lips

Thirsty, in the desert of reality,
For the recurring vision of the rebirth

Of that precious evaporated mirage.

Reflections on the movie Atonement.

UNE AUTRE VIE, UNE AUTRE FOIS

Reflets de pensées mouillées
Survolant les premières vapeurs de rosée printanière.

Images striées fugitives, la nuit, sur le pare-brise.

Restants envoûtants de cette voix,
Durant la lecture d'un journal solitaire,

Sur un banc isolé avec l'apparente sensation
D'une chair invisible sur une chair toute seule.

À l'horloge, il est moins quelque chose.
Le moment fut. Et n'existe plus.

La physique et les minutes sont ce qu'elles sont,
Et nos besoins ne pourront jamais déformer leurs lois en notre faveur.

Les électrons morts et les molécules mourantes
Ne contiennent qu'une solidité sourde.

Alors que sous la patine d'un fatalisme rationnel,
Notre cœur croit toujours pouvoir discerner
Tout un monde rempli d'autres choses :

Le grouillement de la vie dans un étang fait de rêves.

Là, où dans ses profondeurs, l'espoir humain…
…et seul l'espoir humain déluré,

A le courage de respirer l'illusion narcotique de la délusion.

Cette deuxième autre chance
D'une autre vie. Une autre fois.
Qui pend avec séduction près des lèvres gercées

Assoiffées, dans le désert de la réalité,
De la vision récurrente de la renaissance

De ce mirage précieux évaporé.

Réflexions sur le film Atonement.

HAPPINESS MADE OF WHITE

White sun drenched happiness
Cleansed of the heaviness of the absurd.

Meaningfulness imprinted on the soul
With the balm of precious tenderness.

Weightlessness on the left arm
Of trembling anticipation.

The presence of a sparrow.
A gently opening cocoon maybe.

Nervous joy in the late warm wind
Under a conspiring October sun.

Gathered, with loving glances,
On this magic day full of sweet sour ritual,

For the release into the blue crystal sky
Of the Limoges porcelain soul taking flight.

Of a white silk butterfly.

October 14, 2008
A father walking his daughter to her future.

Illustration by Katy Norman

BONHEUR FAIT DE BLANC

Bonheur se noyant dans la blancheur ensoleillée
Nettoyé de la pesanteur de l'absurde.

La signification des choses imprimée sur l'âme
Grâce au baume d'une précieuse tendresse.

Légèreté au bras gauche
D'une anticipation frémissante.

La présence d'une hirondelle.
Un cocon s'ouvrant gentiment peut être.

Joie nerveuse dans une brise tiède tardive
Sous un soleil d'octobre conspirateur.

Assemblés, le regard affectueux,
Ce jour magique rempli de rituel aigre-doux,

Pour l'envol dans un ciel cristallin bleu,
De l'âme en porcelaine de Limoges,

D'un papillon en soie blanche.

Le 14 octobre, 2008
Un père guidant sa fille vers son futur.

THE MAGIC NECKLACE

Between the links bending and folding upon her flesh,
Now lives this necklace.

The cavities next to the bluish emeralds
Let themselves be possessed by the innocent down of her neck.

A scene of happy depravity hides itself
Under the translucent blouse collar.

From time to time the clasp would pull on her skin
As a reminder, to her, of its intimate presence.

Precisely at the instant of her answer, void of conviction,
To a question from the inquisitorial eyes of the committee,

Confused upon seeing in her glance,
Sighs from yesterday.

High powered executive daydreaming during a meeting.

LE COLLIER MAGIQUE

Entre ses anneaux qui se plient et se tordent sur sa chair
Vit maintenant ce collier.

Les cavités près des émeraudes bleuâtres
Se laissent posséder par le duvet innocent de son cou.

Une scène de dépravation joyeuse se cache
Sous le col translucide du chemisier.

De temps à autre les chaînons tirent sur sa peau
Pour lui faire rappeler de leur présence intime.

Précisément au moment où elle répond sans conviction
À une demande des yeux inquisitoriaux du comité

Confus de distinguer dans son regard
Un soupir d'hier.

Sous-directrice pendant une réunion de conseil.

ESPRESSO ROYAL

"Expresso Royal." He then corrected his French inflection to:
"Espresso Royal. What's in a name?" He whispered, to himself.

Not much, it's, rather… who has touched these walls.
This presence. Her presence. Her absence.

Like the good old days, she was still there,
In his mind, to guide his glance.

Not the daily routine
Of bouncing ideas off of each other:

"Cet adjective? Qu'est-ce que tu en penses?"

Not the knee against knee immediacy.
But rather the cold cyberspace replacement.
That must be satisfied now by these four walls.

Seemingly absolute dichotomy,
Between the prosaic and the sublime.

Nothing changes.
The antithetical between the communality,
The anonymity of a wallpaper pealing coffee shop,
And the distilled purity as an emotional symbol.

What must have been in her college years
An evaporation of steam of latte and light conversation.
Sleepy walking breakfast and late night raids for sweets.

Mindless repetition and routine.
Of anxiety, tests, exhaustion,
And anxiety.

_____

All of this, making for an inverted relationship
Between the practicality and emotional value of things.

So, it happens, that mankind
Has sanctified mundane places over the centuries.
That is… mounds of dirt, muddy hills,

Tortuous river banks and quiet tree groves,

That would become settings for smoky temples.
Babel-like basilicas.
Settings for beliefs and eternalized knowledge.

That is how we impose privilege
On privileged places.

It makes solid, the vaporous.
It makes visual, the transparent.
It brings to arm's length what is gone.

And so it came to be,
That in a noisy, coffee house,
With shaky tables legs and sticky Formica,

Intrusive conversations and ring tones,
Disinterested neighbors and impatient clientele,

The whole coldness of the world
Was made into a womb like cocoon.

With the warmth and comfort of Egyptian cotton,
By her very presence within these walls,
And the magic simplicity of her simple attachment to them.

Not the wild eyed Romanticism of years past.
Not this present lyrical reconstruction of things gone.

But rather, just the intellectual solidity,
The personal and shameless self satisfaction,

Of knowing once and for all
That THIS PLACE, of all the things of the past of past,
Resides in stoic realization of a truth
Standing up to inevitable oblivion...

Espresso Royal and its mindless noisy echoes... will have to do.

Everyone's memories of our favorite college coffee shop.

DESERT FLOWER

This flower, near death,
Was trying to suck the last crystals of nourishment
From the dry and abandoned minerals.

And, in its feverish mind,
It still could taste the limpid tropical rains of yesterday.

Her petals had been caressed
By sensual warm mist.

The invading moist breath from the cool hills
Had wrapped itself around its stem and possessed her.

The early spring winds
Had shaken her being to its very core.

So much so, that at times the young swollen pollen
Would fly into space.

Life and future life were at their most vibrant
And nothing but the sap of joy ran into its fibers.

Pure abandonment to the living moment.
Her shinny leaves had been wildly spread
To absorb the solar presence.

And then, from the cold clouds
…from over there…

From the scary places
That we learn to fear before closing our eyes at night,

Those spaces in our mind
That make us afraid of being too happy,

Deep in the ugliness of living
In a changing and dying world,

The things and plants around her withered away

112

And *she* was left
With a still feverish mind and a craving thirst,

With only… in her memory,
The taste of limpid tropical drops of yesterday.

Memories of youth.

ON A BENCH

On Place des Vosges, lives a bench.
It is the bench of remembrance
That makes you unaware of the noises of the city.

This old bench absorbs the past through its cracks
In what used to be the wood of an enchanted forest.

An old man with snowy eyes sits eternally on it.

The birds and children know him.
Hopping, chirping, game balls and shouts,
All respect his universe.

Under the dusty leaves, in the Summer,
Feet in remaining sediment of puddles, in October.
He is: on Place des Vosges.

Not far, Victor Hugo thought of great things.
He, reconstructs minuscule visions,
Genesis of a more intimate reality.

Instead of grandiose Romantic Epics
The old man, on wood hardened by yearning,
Remains serene in front of children's games
On the glazy mud of the moment.

He feels only Love and Need,
Satisfaction and Solitude.

The weakened January sun
Cannot cool an old lubricity.

Among the invisible arms of a woman,
He knows once more the ultimate: to be loved.

The birds remain nervous at his knees:
Trembling with cold and years respectively.

A little boy holding tight to his mother's index:
"Mommy! The Man is talking to a beautiful Lady!"

"Don't say stupid things," says she.

« Et la mer efface sur le sable les pas des amants désunis »
Lyrics by Jacques Prévert. Yves Montand's version.

Illustration by Katy Norman.

SUR UN BANC

Place des Vosges, existe un banc.
C'est le banc aux souvenirs
Qui rend sourd aux bruits de la ville.

Ce vieux banc absorbe le passé à travers ses craquelures
Dans ce qui fut le bois d'une forêt magique.
Un vieil homme aux yeux enneigés y est éternellement assis.

Les oiseaux et les enfants le connaissent.
Sautillements, piaillements, ballons et cris,
Respectent son univers.

À l'ombre des feuilles poussiéreuses, l'été,
Les pieds dans les restants vaseux des flaques, en octobre
Il est : Place des Vosges.

Pas loin, Victor Hugo pensait en grand,
Lui, il se représente des images minuscules
Genèse d'une réalité intime.

Au lieu de grandioses épopées romantiques
Le vieillard sur le bois durci par les soupirs
Reste impassible devant les jeux d'enfants
Sur la terre glaise du moment.

Il ne ressent qu'amour et envie,
Satisfaction et solitude.

Le soleil bas de janvier
Ne parvient pas à refroidir une ancienne lubricité.

Dans les bras invisibles d'une femme,
Il reconnaît une fois de plus l'ultime : être aimé.

Les oiseaux restent nerveux près de ses genoux :
Tremblant de froid et d'âge respectivement.

Un petit garçon tenant l'index de sa maman :
«Dis maman ! Le monsieur parle à une belle dame !»

«Ne dis pas de bêtises, » répond-t-elle.

FORBIDDEN FRUIT

It was the elegance, the tenderness of the rejection,
That kept him convinced to the very end
Of her worthiness of his love.

She was generous of heart and pure of mind
In setting unwelcome boundaries.

Accidental fluttering of her knee,
Semi platonic skimming of her face,
Met with the beginnings of puritanical reflexes.

Emotional survival, clarity of mores
Were taking charge of unregulated drives.

And whether in a cavernous frigid hall of a medieval castle,
Or separated by a stern stick shift overlooking a lake,

The gesture was historic and proper.
Repeated and repeatable.

Expected and respectful.
And eternally hurtful.

She had become… untouchable.

Thus, on the other side
Of what was his existential decision,

Existed what delineated his freedom of action…

…her legitimate claim to earthly happiness.

That is where he learned,
That is when he knew,

That the luscious fruit, its flagrance,
Fleshy pulp and raspy taste,

Was as real and present
As was his remaining passion.

But would live henceforth
On separated sides of that reality.

Reflections on Lancelot and Guinevere.

FRUIT DÉFENDU

Ce fut l'élégance, la tendresse de son rejet,
Qui le convainquirent jusqu'au bout
Qu'elle était digne de son amour.

Elle était généreuse de cœur et pure d'esprit
Alors qu'elle établissait des limites.

Effleurement accidentel de son genou,
Frôlement quasi platonique de son visage,
Retenus par les premiers temps de réflexes puritains.

La survie émotionnelle, la clarté de moeurs
Prenaient la relève de soifs jusque là gratuites.

Et que cela se passa dans une énorme pièce d'un château médiéval,
Ou bien avec vue sur un lac et séparés par un levier de vitesse,

Le geste était historique et correct.
Répété et répétable.

Attendue et respectable.
Et éternellement douloureux.

Elle était devenue… intouchable.

Donc, de l'autre côté
De ce qui était, pour lui, une décision existentielle,

Existait ce qui délimitait sa liberté de choix…

…le droit légitime à un bonheur terrestre de cette femme.

C'est là qu'il apprit,
C'est alors qu'il sut,

Que ce fruit savoureux, son parfum,
Sa chair onctueuse et son goût râpeux,

Était aussi vrai et présent
Que ce qu'il sentait des restants de sa passion.

Mais que ceux-là vivront dorénavant
Chacun de leur propre côté de cette réalité.

Réflexions sur Lancelot et Geneviève.

IN THE SHADE OF A FLOWER

Like detecting the subtle aroma
Of her favorite spice in a complex sauce.

Like hearing the quasi feminine solo
Of her favorite male singer mixed in with other songs.

Like the shock of mistakenly recognizing
Her virile voice among others behind you at the coffee shop.

All of these are found in the cacophony
Of the extraneous baggage of daily life.

Loved pieces of the Universe following us restlessly.

Ironically it is from what is small and diminutive,
What is retreating and respectful,

It is from what hides inside the obvious,
It is deep under the blanket of protection
...from the pain of remembrance...

That the richness and multiplicity
Of tangible morsels of happiness and sighs

Reemerge, one day, when we least expect them.
The body and the mind are indeed the poet's temple.

In it, the divinities have given us
The language of symbols and synesthesia

That make one... sunsets and flesh.
Scent and person. Perfume and moment.

Allowing the impossible to exist.
Making the past walk again next to us.

And so, although he was in the middle
Of the sterile hardness of an urban sidewalk,

Although the evaporation

Of diesel and hot-dogs was nauseating,

Although he was late again for that meeting,
Although it was late in his life,

Vapors of the essence of the natural, organic,
Sun blessed presence of the accidental smell of a flower

Invaded his being.

After all these years, after all the distance,
She was still inside of him.

"If some one loves a flower, of which just one single blossom grows in all the millions and millions of stars, it is enough to make him happy just to look at the stars. He can say to himself, 'Somewhere, my flower is there. ...She cast her fragrance and her radiance over me.'"

"Said the fox... 'To me, you are still nothing more than a little boy who is just like a hundred thousand other little boys. And I have no need of you. And you, on your part, have no need of me. To you, I am nothing more than a fox like a hundred thousand other foxes. But if you tame me, then we shall need each other. To me, you will be unique in all the world. To you, I shall be unique in all the world...'"

"'I am beginning to understand,' said the little prince. 'There is a flower... I think that she has tamed me...'"

The Little Prince, *Antoine de Saint Exupéry.*

À L'OMBRE D'UNE FLEUR

Comme l'on retrouve l'arôme subtil
De son épice favorite dans une sauce compliquée.

Comme l'on entend le solo quasi féminin,
Mélangé à tant d'autres, de son chanteur mâle favori.

Comme le choque de croire, à tort,
Que la voix virile derrière nous était la sienne.

Toutes ces choses errent dans la cacophonie
Des rapports gratuits de la vie quotidienne.

Ce sont nos morceaux préférés d'un univers
Qui nous poursuivent sans répit.

Ironiquement, c'est...
De ce qui est petit et diminutif,

De ce qui est timide et qui nous respecte,
De ce qui se cache à nos yeux,

Dessous sa couverture protectrice
Contre la douleur du souvenir,

Que... la richesse et la multiplicité,
Que... des morceaux tangibles de bonheur et de soupirs,
Ressortent, un jour, quant on s'y attend le moins.

Le corps et l'esprit étant, vraiment, le temple du poète.

En lui, les divinités nous offrent
Le langage des symboles et de la synesthésie.

Faisant un... des soleils couchants et de la chair.
Du parfum et de la personne. De l'essence et du moment.

Permettant à l'impossible d'exister.
Recréant sa présence à nos côtés.

———————————————

123

Et alors qu'il se trouvait au milieu
De la dure stérilité d'un trottoir urbain,

Alors que les vapeurs
De diesel et de hot-dogs donnaient la nausée,

Alors qu'il était une fois de plus en retard pour ce rendez-vous,
Alors qu'il se faisait tard dans sa vie,

Les nuages vaporeux de la présence solaire,
Naturelle et organique, d'une fleur rencontrée au hasard,

Envahit son corps.

Après toutes ces années, après tout ce voyage,
Elle était toujours en lui.

"If some one loves a flower, of which just one single blossom grows in all the millions and millions of stars, it is enough to make him happy just to look at the stars. He can say to himself, 'Somewhere, my flower is there. ...She cast her fragrance and her radiance over me.'"

"Said the fox... 'To me, you are still nothing more than a little boy who is just like a hundred thousand other little boys. And I have no need of you. And you, on your part, have no need of me. To you, I am nothing more than a fox like a hundred thousand other foxes. But if you tame me, then we shall need each other. To me, you will be unique in all the world. To you, I shall be unique in all the world...'"

"'I am beginning to understand,' said the little prince. 'There is a flower... I think that she has tamed me...'"

The Little Prince, *Antoine de Saint Exupéry.*

IT HAD BEEN A LONG TIME SINCE...

It had been a long time since he had not contemplated,
In the limitless intimate abyss of the brown of the iris,
The reflection of the last flames of his virility.

Long ago that the intoxicating buzzing of the labial sounds,
Whispered next to his ears,
Had made him deaf to the inconsequential other noises of life.

It occurred to him that in that past,
All had been only perfumes.
Purity and unforgettable essences.
Reserve. Embers and authenticity.

Having taken a drink in her very being:
Of things, which, with only the fluidity of their value and passion,

Had tried to contradict
The dumb opaque material presence of the inevitable.

————————————————————

Like these Medieval monks,
In the moist asceticism of their cells,

Ceaselessly repeating their burning and sacred litanies
For fear of losing their religious fervor
Caused by the cooling of cherished moments,

He would retell loved and loving words,
As though they might, by the very weight of their presence,

Have recreated the curves of the back
And the honesty of the glance.

Alone now in front of his eternal present and his daily newspaper,
His mind turned to those days:
...a thought... an envy.

In this past, he heard himself whisper:

"All had been only perfumes.

Purity and unforgettable essences.
Reserve. Embers and authenticity."

Reflections on:
L'invitation au voyage, *by Charles Baudelaire*

« Là, tout n'est qu'ordre et beauté,
Luxe, calme et volupté. »

"There, all is only order and beauty
Luxury, calmness and voluptuousness."

and

Chéri, *by Colette*

Léa, saying her farewells to her much younger lover:

« Tu as dit tout cela, tu as pensé tout cela de moi ? J'étais donc si belle à tes yeux, dis ? Si bonne ? À l'âge où tant de femmes ont fini de vivre, j'étais pour toi la plus belle, la meilleure des femmes, et tu m'aimais ? Comme je te remercie, mon chéri... »

"You said all that, you thought all that of me? I had been so beautiful in your eyes, tell me? So good to you? At an age when women have stopped living, I had been the most, the best of women, and you loved me? How grateful I am to you darling..."

IL Y AVAIT LONGTEMPS...

Il y avait longtemps qu'il n'avait contemplé,
Dans l'intimité de l'abysse sans limite du marron de l'iris,
Le reflet des dernières flammes de sa virilité.

Longtemps que le frôlement enivrant du son des labiales,
Murmurées près de son oreille,
L'avait rendu sourd aux bruits inconséquents de la vie.

Il se rendit compte que dans ce passé,
Tout n'avait été que parfum,
Essence pure et inoubliable.
Pudeur, braise et authenticité.

Ayant bu en elle les choses, qui, avec seulement la limpidité de leur
valeur et passion,
Avaient essayé de contredire le minerai opaque bête de l'inévitable.

Comme ces moines médiévaux, dans l'ascétisme de leurs cellules
suintantes
Répétant leurs litanies, brûlantes et sacrées, de peur de perdre la ferveur
De moments si chers qui s'attiédissent.

Il se redisait les paroles aimées et aimantes,
Comme si elles pouvaient, du poids de leur présence,
Reconstruire les rondeurs de ses reins et la franchise de son regard.

Seul maintenant devant son présent éternel et son journal du matin,
Il eut sur son passé... une pensée... une envie.

Dans ce passé, se murmura-t-il,
Tout n'avait été que parfum,
Essence pure et inoubliable.
Pudeur, braise et authenticité.

« Là, tout n'est qu'ordre et beauté,
Luxe, calme et volupté. »
L'invitation au voyage.

Léa, le personnage dans Chéri de Colette, disant ses adieux à son jeune amant :
«Tu as dit tout cela, tu as pensé tout cela de moi ? J'étais donc si belle à tes yeux, dis ? Si
bonne ? À l'âge où tant de femmes ont fini de vivre, j'étais pour toi la plus belle, la meilleure
des femmes, et tu m'aimais ? Comme je te remercie, mon chéri...»

127

EPILOGUE

LAST GLANCE
(e.g. In the Shade of a Flower)

Since that night, on that darkened highway, he had used words, just words, as though they had been a translucent lace. And the knowing topography of the lace had solid and empty spaces that held them magically one to the other. Only his heart could have given source to such fine filigrees.

His words had come slipping out, still warm and surrounded with the glue of life. They had come out with almost no effort on his part: practically without contractions and pain. The birthing of authenticity.

He covered his solitary moments with this grammatical balm and all was well. He rubbed really hard this lyrical substance into the wounds caused by the voids of his soul; thus hoping to cure himself of the palpitations following the absence of things and people of the past.

He easily wrote about literary fantasies, about Santa Claus and grandiose Faustian oaths. He wrote about Proustian essences and lyrical reconstructions in some Parisian cemetery.

And although he felt at ease and proud in the down of his words; although he felt protected from reality by a selfish artistic intoxication; although he manipulated the antitheses by mining the historical and biblical landscapes: he whispered to himself:

"All I ever wanted, all we basically want in life is the daily, earthly, human solidity of companionship: such simple solidity, as a door closing behind us, of the sound of a crusty baguette, of the exotic and symbolic emanations of a couscous."

"All these years of study; all these philosophies and philosophers. And becoming convinced that the absurd is more deadly afraid of that crusty baguette."

"Voltaire was correct in fighting the intolerance in this world with a vegetable garden."

Having no readily available tool, it came about that it was with words that he had tried to recreate some of his cherished visions. Visions of shades of a favorite black cloth and the solidity of a glance on him as it disappeared into the materiality of the metallic traffic around them.

It is thus with words that he has tried to rebuilt the moments.

In the middle of Things where she and all these visions were no longer, there was, many times, the odor of death coming from the danger of anti-lyricism.

The Antichrist for the artist.

He feared the smells of the lack of inspiration that is so similar to the stench of road kills. The smells of perverted and diabolical fantasies that make the mind contemplate the destruction of the written word. He felt a multitude of emotions, of jealousy, of hate: a feeling of sterility in front of his efforts to put her back in his arms on that dance floor.

He no longer wanted these pieces of paper that dared to put themselves at her level. Not a second of her glance could be replaced by them. He was left with using, far from her, what they both had become: the plasticity of words on the screen in front of a plastic keyboard.

Words had become the instruments manipulated in a private and shameful chamber away from prying eyes, as he thought about all these things. He often felt, in this hidden effort, that his lyrical seminal essence had been lost without fertilizing anything. His thoughts, he feared, would remain like stains on lush and thick paper made, unfortunately, of dead cellulose. He was left with caressing the past with only words.

He came to understand Rimbaud's temptation to stop writing. It must have been his way to put an end to the building toxicity of dark thoughts. The same that speak of adored things and moments but without any hope of seeing them once more. Only streams of acidity, it seemed, could now come out of what used to be source of sweet water. Having looked for pleasure and its easy gratuitous acquisition in the impressionism of youth, he now feared that the former defined itself better by its very absence.

And so, all this brought him to the ultimate glance upon these precious pieces of desire that he concluded had been the key to the only human scale measure of the eternity of things.

Such seemingly insignificant moments symbolized by the contact of the left ear on the chest of the only being that meant anything.

Moments during which he still could recognize in the same protecting maternal glance in the arms of his lover, the one of his childhood fevers.

Moments that will flash back upon his death where he will know for certain that all will be fine: as he gives back to the universe its part of what is left in his lungs. This universe will shrink into a tunnel vision where will be seen, as one: the face of the mother, the sister and the lover.

At that very moment a recall will automatically and corporally come back to him. It is a scene in the blackness of a blackened bedroom.

He opens his eyes and begins to pray, only to realize afterwards, to his surprise, that he has not said anything. That is when he notices that his very body does not allow itself to believe any longer in this fantasy. It does not allow him to believe in the eternal father while his own is dying at the cancerous rhythm of the creaking of the mattress springs in the bedroom next to his.

He attempts to pray once more.

It is the end.

Never again will he know the quiet world of things that gently follow each other in an orchestrated composition.

Never again.

Instead, a deep unease takes over. It is the feeling that at any moment dangerous things could swallow gratuitously and by pure cruelty all that he loves in an infernal and noisy cacophony.

Until the day, until the day of that glance, of the dance on this floor, in front of the lavender fields, at the top of Montmartre and next to the Corniche. A day when burning red lips and an intelligent glance transfixed everything. To know that this glance, on all the things that he has loved, will speak for him and that a sort of eternity exits in it through his reconstruction of them.

It is in a self-constructed world with no absolutes; a world with moments of intellectual arrogance; a world happy away from irrational things; ex-nihilo; a world outside of and safe from the jealous reach of divine references:

"It is in such a world," he whispers, "that I condemned myself to exist."

And it is, ironically, in this precise world that he believes, for what seems to be the first time, since a long time.

He continues:

"I believe that Things are the way they are because Things wanted it so in their unintelligent, inevitable way."

And so he submits to them while reciting under his breath the creed of the solitary lover:

"It is in the very fragility of the sound of a chance glance that I have found the eternity of Things."

His fingers were clenched on the steering wheel of his car...

With "Say It Isn't So," by Hall & Oates, playing in the background...

GLOSSARY

This glossary of words, names and terms is added for the convenience of readers to enhance their enjoyment of and access to the full range of language and meaning used in this book. Many of Jean-Yves Solinga's poems are translations from French and are littered with words of particular cultural and literary reference from this language. There are also philosophical, religious and historical references and other terms, which may be unfamiliar to some readers. The briefest definition or explanation is provided only to support the meaning within the poetry. Of course alternative definitions exist and these can be found in any good dictionary, thesaurus or encyclopedia. The glossary is presented in alphabetical order to avoid the need to repeat words that appear in more than one poem.

Baies des Anges: Bay of the Angels, City of Nice on the Côte d'Azur in Southern France along which runs the boulevard of La Promenade des Anglais.

Baudelaire, Charles: French writer known for his seminal collection of poems *Flowers of Evil*. Beautiful and timeless poetry about guilt, lust and urban Paris of the nineteenth century. "Le Spleen" was supposed to be the source of a general melancholia.

Bécaud, Gilbert: Popular composer and singer of romantic and lyrical songs.

Bergman, Ingmar: Swedish movie director of the nightmares that can be human relations.

Bled: Arabic term for a field. Often used in French to denote the void of the dry panorama of North Africa.

Camargue: Delta of the Rhône river where the armies of the Crusades were assembled.

Camus, Albert: Philosopher of the Absurd. Also wrote the play *Caligula* of a demented Caesar obsessed among other things with acquiring the impossible.

Carafes: A wide-mouthed glass or metal bottle with a lip or spout, for holding and serving beverages.

Chitane: Satan in Arabic.

Colette: French writer who captured the feminine psychology and issues in the man's world of the early Twentieth Century.

Doubleganger: A double or a split of a personality used for literary effect.

Église Saint Laurent: A Roman-Provincial church in Marseille, destroyed by German soldiers in 1943. Oncle Jules' painting is of the original.

Flaubert, Gustave: One of world literature's great. He views the beauty of language and analysis of the human heart, as the drive of art.

Glance: (also referred to as "The Gaze" or "The Look") Jean-Paul Sartre defined "The Glance" within the framework of his concepts of Existential Philosophy. The following quotes encapsulate his views. From *L'être et le néant* (*Being and Nothingness*): "We are who we are only in the eyes of other people and their looks are what make us come to terms with ourselves as ourselves." From the same source: "My Original Fall is the existence of the Other. And of course, from the character of Garcin in *Huis Clos* (*No Exit*): "No need for a grill, Hell is other people."

Job: God fearing and wealthy biblical figure challenged by various calamities during which he kept his faith in God. Job eventually regained his status and fortune.

Kir: An aperitif of wine and Cassis liqueur.

Lascaux Caves: Caves in South Central France with prehistoric paintings.

Lonesco, Eugène: French playwright of the theatre of the Absurd. He had an uncanny ability of making "concrete" his ideas and philosophy. In *Rhinoceros*, he makes cultural and political oppression appear under these enormous beasts. In *Le roi se meurt* [*Exit the King*] he manages to "concrete" again the "disappearance" of things equate to the act of dying.

Maghreb: In Arabic, the West, the setting sun. North Africa, in particular Morocco, Algeria and Tunisia.

Malefic: Product of evil; malicious.

Manet, Edouard: French Impressionist painter who painted his famous *Olympia*, a very daring treatment of a reclining nude looking directly at the viewer and a stark use of white and technique for her form.

Mephistopheles: The Devil in *Faust* among other places.

Mimosas: Bush producing yellow fluffy spherical flowers in warmer climates.

Noilly Prat: Originally a dry, straw-hued vermouth from Marseillan, in the Hérault département of southern France. Joseph Noilly, a herbalist, developed the first formula in 1813. It was the first example of a dry vermouth and is among the golden, straw and white vermouths generally known as "French

Vermouth".

Other: An existential concept where by the experience of the Other is the experience of another person who inhabits the same world as you do. That Other persons mere presence, or imagined presence, acts to limit or modify your behavior or freedom.

Places des Vosges: Beautiful square in the middle of lovely brick buildings. Favorite setting for strolling and park bench reading.

Prévert, Jacques: French lyricist, composer and poet. Wrote some of the most memorable lyrics to iconic French songs, such as: "Autumn Leaves."

Proust, Marcel: French author who wrote one of literature's better known passages: the unsolicited "remembrance" of the past while eating les madeleines, cookies that he would have with tea as a child.

Rimbaud, Arthur: A precocious and extremely talented and troubled nineteenth century French poet.

Sagan, Françoise: An assertive feminist in the years after World War II who was not afraid to use her frank analysis of women's view of unconventional sexual relationships in her novels. *Un certain sourire* was her first explosive novel.

Sartres, Jean-Paul: French philosopher who popularized the concepts of Existentialism. The Glance (Gaze or Look) of the Other plays a great role in is criticism in how we define ourselves.

Sidi Moussa: Little beach north of Salé in Morocco. On its cliffs are a "Marabout," a pilgrimage structure to the holy man Moses and a fort.

Sisyphus: A king in classical mythology who offended Zeus and was punished in Hades by being forced to roll an enormous boulder to the top of a steep hill. Every time the boulder neared the top, it always escaped him and rolling down forcing him to start again.

Soylent Green: Haunting science fiction movie of a future with an exploding population and a nonexistent nature. One of the character's option is to commit suicide while watching prohibited images of that long ago past.

Synesthesia: A condition in which one type of stimulation evokes the sensation of another, as when the hearing of a sound produces the visualization of a color.

Totems: Symbols and presences, physical or others, in cultures studied by sociologists and anthropologists to explain their mores and beliefs.

TITLES AND FIRST LINES

Titles are in italics, first lines are in regular text.

A Devine Indictment	52
* *À L'ombre D'une Fleur*	123
Alexis de Tocqueville, Revisited	40
Alternate Universe	68
And now… something really important:	79
Angular pieces from the previously whole	46
Another Life Another Time	104
Another nonchalant glance to the left, in a routine moment:	83
At Ease With Oneself	80
At Least We Were Thin	56
At times, like multicolored butterfly wings	80
Beginnings… and the End	81
"Better a smart critic than a dumb friend."	40
Between the links bending and folding upon her flesh,	108
Black and white memory	56
* *Bonheur Fair de Blanc*	107
Bonheur se noyant dans la blancheur ensoleillée	107
Ce fut l'élégance, la tendresse de son rejet,	119
Ce jour-là, après le déjeuner, le bonheur et la satisfaction	77
Cela se passa à la Porte du charme et de la joie,	93
C'était plutôt l'incongru du site.	102
Chitane	58
* *Chitane [originally written in French]*	60
Cloué au parquet de la passivité, il se voit en l'Autre.	96
Comme l'on retrouve l'arôme subtil.	123
Desert Flower	112
Don't Look Back	67
Droplets of Time	101
* *Effort Pour Remédier aux Choses*	93
Emotional Price	49
Emotional Voyeurism	95
Entre ses anneaux qui se plient et se tordent sur sa chair	109
Espresso Royal	110
Exit the King or Learning How To Die Properly	27

"Expresso Royal." He then corrected his French inflection to: 110

First Snow and Big Bang   35
Forbidden Fruit   117
From the last frozen vapor crystals   52
* *Fruit Défendu*   119

Gentle souls of the world, unite and multiply.   84
Girl From a Small New England Town   43
Golden or silver metal objects on the shoulders.   23
* *Gouttelettes du Temps Passé*   102

Happiness and contentment disguised themselves   76
Happiness Made of White   106
Happy Thoughts   37
Haiti: From Barbeque to Misery   24
High School Number   25
His mother had warned him: 58
How to Waste Your life   88

* *Il y Avait Longtemps… [originally written in French]*   127
Il y avait longtemps qu'il n'avait contemplé,   127
In the true definition of the definition of oneself,   68
In the Third Person   70
In the Shade of a Flower   121
In her college days was this seat.   43
Ima   42
Imperceptible sighs from the object of desire   97
It Had Been a Long Time Since…   125
It had been a long time since he had not contemplated,   125
It happened at the Gate of Appeal and Joy,   91
It takes religious courage for love   21
It was better than most other times   57
It was morning and the sun was setting.   89
It was the elegance, the tenderness of the rejection,   117
It was the incongruity of the setting.   101

Late December remnants of searing Summer heat.   35
* *Le Collier Magique [originally written in French]*   109
* *Les mimosas*   77
Like a toggle switch in his mind   86
Like detecting the subtle aroma   121

Lying to Oneself   21

Manifesto for Gentle Souls   84
Memorial Day Fantasy   55
Mimosas   76
Multiple nuances of whites   62
Multitude of ancestral possibilities   81

Nailed to the floor of passivity, he sees himself in the Other.   95
Nous nous trompons, vivant nos vies   32
Nothing is free.   49
Nuances multiples de blancheurs   63

Of Biblical Ancestry and Nude Beaches   78
On a Bench   114
Oncle Jules   57
On Place des Vosges, lives a bench.   114

Personal, intimate horizons becoming more and more limited.   27
Philosophy in a Garage   39
Picturing her standing   72
Place des Vosges, existe un banc.   116
Primordial cry of wounded hunter in the Savannahs
                                        of our opening years.   42

Quilt: All This Wisdom on a Bed   46

Reciprocal Visions   83
Reflections of moist thoughts   104
Reflections on Olympia by Manet   62
Reflets de pensées mouillées   105
* *Réflexions sur l'Olympia de Manet [originally written in French]*   63
Remembrance of Spring Grass   86

Sa mère l'avait prévenu :   60
Silence, respectful silence.   55
* *Si Proche… et si Loin [originally written in French]*   99
Sitting on a snow covered picnic bench,   103
So Close and Yet So Far   97
Somewhere in the recombined air mixture of the future,   65
Soupirs imperceptibles de l'objet de désir   99
* *Sur un Banc [originally written in French]*   116

Syntax in a letter that reflects back to its surprised reader.   70

Test of a Contemporary Job on Wall Street   53
The everyday marvel of the marvel of everyday.   66
The gun barrel   47
The Granite Wall   85
The Keyboard   72
The Lascaux Caves   65
The Magic Necklace   108
The other side of the granite wall,   85
The shyness of the moon came out last night   88
The Taste of Snow   103
The Teacher... a Cultivated Nomad   64
The teacher is a cultivated nomad   64
There came into his heart   53
The very picture of living in the moment: 67
This flower, near death,   112
To Live in the Moment   66
* *Totems de L'univers*   32
Totems of the Universe   29
Trying to Undo Things   91

Ultimate Philosophical Delusion   23
* *Une Autre vie,Une Autre Fois*   105
Upon a Funeral Parlor   20

View From the Tip of Foreign Policies   47
Voyage: Making the best of Things   89
* *Voyeurisme Émotionnel*   96

We mistakenly live our lives within the hardened pieces   29
What if we... this world...   37
What Really Counts   79
Where everything will end,   20
White sun drenched happiness   106
Wild open spaces of untamed passions: 78
With a Greek Chorus background   39

You have to be proud of mankind   24
Young couple on the uneven urban sidewalk.   25

www.ingramcontent.com/pod-product-compliance
Lightning Source LLC
Chambersburg PA
CBHW080532090426
42733CB00015B/2561